'SUPER NEURO YOU'

ACHIEVE MORE SUCCESS FOR LESS STRESS AND
MAKE A DIFFERENCE FOR YOURSELF AND OTHERS.

CLAIRE WALTON

DEDICATION

To my beautiful daughter, Emily. Without you I may have gone mad over the years.

You inspire me to want to be my Highest Potential Self and to Make A Difference every day, for myself, for you, for all others I connect with.

You are my 10th Superpower!

CONTENTS

DISCLAIMER

I am not a therapist but use some techniques from therapy. If anything you read in this book or practise from this book triggers any difficult emotions that may be associated with T–trauma, you should consult a qualified trauma professional.

Feel free to contact me on claire@leadersaremad.co.uk for referrals.

Enjoy reading and good luck on your journey to finding your *Super Neuro You*.

INTRODUCTION

Why this book is for you

If you want to achieve your Highest Potential Self (HPS) and access your true ability to achieve more success for less stress, you will benefit from this book.

This book is for you if:

- You ever feel stuck in an exhausting pattern of behaviour.
- You know you have more to offer but don't have the energy to offer it.
- You hold on to the past, worry about the future and miss out on the present.
- You know parts of you sabotage your success, happiness and health and you want to relate to them more effectively.

- You want to be the most positive role model for your children or the people you lead.
- You want to learn how to manage your superpower zappers and boost your superpowers to become the best version of you.
- You are prepared to invest in a journey of self-discovery, to learn new techniques and to practise, practise, practise.

You will learn some of the fundamentals of becoming your Highest Potential Self. I apply these to myself and use them with clients. You will experience them through the fictional character of Laura Masters. Laura is a fictional composite of myself and many of my coaching clients of different genders. You are introduced to Laura at a point in her life when she decides to work with a Coach (Me – lucky Laura). She wants to understand why she keeps getting in the way of her true potential in life, health and happiness. Instead of being exhausted by the strain of having a successful career, she wants to achieve more success across her whole life and for less stress.

I want to have some fun with this book just as I do in my work. Being playful and using humour to lighten our approach help us to learn more effectively. I love Wonder Woman, and throughout adult life I have come to love the concept behind superheroes. I have referenced links to superheroes in this book. For me, the superhero is all things human. They are vulnerable to life's challenges, they have weaknesses, they need support from others and ultimately they achieve more as a team or tribe.

I would like this book to enable you to connect with your "HPS" and to encourage you to talk to others about what resonates with you as you read this book. We learn more when we learn with others, sharing our thoughts and experiences aloud. We learn when we listen to the insights and actions of others. If you are interested in exploring further the concepts in this book go onto www.leadersaremad. co.uk to find details for next 'Super Neuro You' group coaching programme.

I am writing this book during the Covid-19 pandemic. This has brought home to us all the importance of self-care and the ripple effect of looking after our mental, emotional and physical health. *Super Neuro You* will positively influence the people you connect with: family, friends, colleagues and people in your community. It is my hope that *Super Neuro You* is positively contagious, creating a huge ripple effect of positive change. Now that is MAD!

How this book works

In Chapter One you will meet Laura Masters, an Executive Director in her mid-forties. Whilst successful, in many ways she does not feel as though she is living up to her potential in life. Laura shares her story with you through entries in her journal. By reading Laura's account of her life at the start of her journal you will get an insight into why she wants to work with a Coach. However, as with most coaching clients, Laura's initial reasons for coaching hide the many benefits transformational coaching will bring her.

In Chapter Two Laura meets the coach for the first time in a 'Chemistry Meeting' (Coach/Client chemistry is critical to success). In this chapter you will also be introduced to the voice of the Coach (me) through excerpts of dialogue from the meeting. During the Chemistry session the Coach explains her coaching approach to Laura. She begins to share some of the neuroscience of change, a theme further developed as Laura continues through her coaching journey. Throughout the book you will move from reading Laura's journal in which she reflects on life, to her sessions with the Coach and to her attempts to practise the techniques the Coach shares with her.

Chapters Two to Seven bring to life several different coaching sessions Laura has with the Coach. They take place over seven months and are represented by excerpts of dialogue from some of the coaching sessions that Laura has as part of her transition. Laura shares some of how she puts the coaching into practice as she transitions from an exhausted yet successful woman who isn't happy with her life to a happy and healthy woman who is ready to become a role model for success without the compromise of exhaustion.

In Chapter Eight you will see Laura three years on from the initial coaching. Once again she records in her journal what is happening in her life. You will hear how Laura is achieving her vision of true success and some of her critical lessons along the way.

The final Chapter is a few words from my perspective on helping clients like Laura.

You can read this book purely for pleasure and interest or you can choose to try some, or all of the exercises experienced by Laura, either in the sessions or as homework. You can use these exercises on your own or find a friend or peer to work through them with you.

You can find the resources in the 'Book Downloads' section of my website.[1] These are left in word format for you to write into the document or print off. They can also be used with your team but must not be distributed further or used for commercial gain.

https://www.leadersaremad.co.uk/super-neuro-you/

Use the password : SuperNeuro2021:)

 To help you identify when an online resource is available you will see this logo

To help you identify when you have homework to complete you will see this icon

Reading the book may inspire you to find a professional Coach to support you on your own journey. If you want to contact me for an initial consultation (Chemistry Meeting) you can do this via the booking page on www.leadersaremad.co.uk

Hopefully you have also bought the 'Super Neuro Me' Journal that compliments this book. Whilst working through the book, as aspects of Laura's journey resonate with you, you will find that making notes in your Journal will help you to keep a record of insights and actions. You can also use the Journal to make notes in response to the exercises you complete and to track your progress. Journals can be ordered from Amazon.

This book is not:

- a guide for Coaches.
- the story of one client but a mixture of clients and me.
- a book about IFS therapy: it describes a coaching approach inspired by IFS techniques.
- a full representation of everything I might cover in

a coaching relationship with a client. It merely represents some aspects of coaching related to achieving more success for less stress.

A bit about me

I am MAD! I have been MAD for a long time, I just didn't realise how MAD I was. I have been Making A Difference to a huge number of people. To family, friends, colleagues and to the hundreds of thousands of employees and millions of customers directly and indirectly impacted by the decisions I have made. Over the past few years, as I have entered mid-life and a career change from Executive Director to Executive and Leadership Coach, I have begun to understand how I could have achieved much more for significantly less stress, pain, suffering and illness. No wonder I am MAD!

I am...

Mother And Daughter

Mum And Dad

Married And Divorced

Masters And Diploma

Manager And Director

Menopausal And Dangerous

Motivated And Distracted

Maybe A Diva

Mentally All Drained

Moody And Depressed

Mentor And Dynamic

Many And Diverse

Mindful And Dreamer

Making A Difference – starting with me!

My struggles have led me to learn through lived experience and a tenacity to understand why things have happened to me and what I can learn from them. They have inspired me to develop my superpowers!

Being curious and compassionate towards myself rather than constantly blaming myself and beating myself up are strengths I have nurtured when no one else was there to nurture me.

I have been courageous and confident. As a woman, working in what has been a male orientated world for most of my career, I have believed in myself and pushed myself forward to demonstrate my worth wherever I have worked. This hasn't always been easy. In fact, it has been quite challenging.

At just 23 I had my daughter, Emily. During the baby and toddler years I was working long hours. I travelled around the South East of England and then the North East of England as a Regional Human Resources Manager for one of the UK's large superstore retailers. I didn't have family support on hand for most of Emily's childhood and my life was mainly a balance between looking after my daughter and working hard at my job and establishing a successful career with several promotions in quick succession.

When Emily was seven years old her father and I divorced. He moved away and I fundamentally raised Emily on my own as a single parent. Emily continued to see her father every other weekend but providing a good home, schooling, childcare and everything else was down to me both logistically and financially. I learnt to be even more organised and clear on my priorities, which were: Emily first, then work and then me. It was stressful. By the time I was in my early 30s I was commuting into London, two hours there and two hours back, juggling a Corporate Change Director role, childcare, school homework, bedtime routines and trying to make sure we had fun on Emily's weekends with me. I think I did okay. This juggling act carried on throughout my career and Emily's school years. We moved several times and I held numerous Executive level Director roles for different companies as I progressed a career as an Interim Executive Director, Management Consultant and Coach.

My career was a success story in many ways. However, it was not without its challenges. I navigated bullying and sexual harassment experiences on more than one occasion. In hindsight, I didn't always handle them well, to the detriment of my mental, emotional and physical health.

I married again sixteen years after my divorce from Emily's father. In the intervening years there were more relationships than I like to admit to. Each one was good for a while and then did not work out for a multitude of reasons. I tend not to regret any of them as each one has since been put under scrutiny and I have learnt so much about myself and what it is to be human.

Unfortunately, my marriage in my late forties was also not to be. Once again, rather than being regretful, I am grateful for the experience. It was the catalyst that brought me to write this book. At the end of this short-lived marriage, I became interested in the subject of Trust: how we build it and how we lose it. It all started with a book I read, then a course of study which introduced me to the field of neuroscience. Since then, I have been further developing in my knowledge and skills to learn as much as I can about how we wonderfully imperfect humans function.

As an Executive and Leadership Performance Coach, I apply what I have learnt through my studies in neuroscience and positive psychology, as well as a variety of coaching and therapy inspired approaches and techniques. My lived experience as a working parent, single parent, woman, and Executive Director working across diverse organisations, also enables me to connect with and support my clients on many different levels.

Despite the juggling, my parenting seems to have been pretty successful. I am proud to say that my daughter is a wonderful 29-year-old woman who studied Clinical Psychology at Masters level, whilst working and volunteering for The Samaritans. It was Emily who inspired me to take a year out from my career and study for my Masters, an MBA at Newcastle University, the same university Emily was studying at. We graduated one day apart and celebrated together. Those days count as two of the proudest of my life. Emily currently works for a large children's charity as a Business Development Manager, having forged a career to date working in sectors which are driven by a core purpose to support those less fortunate than most. She has also qualified as a Life Coach and is starting to help young women navigate those challenging years of early adulthood.

When I look back on the 34 years since my eighteenth birthday, before I started my adult years and the journey ahead, I wish I had known then what I know now. I don't mean I wish I had known what to expect. That would have been boring. I wish I had the knowledge, the skills and the tools to enable me to manage myself more effectively. I wish I had understood how our brains work, how our brains are more than just the physical structure in our skulls and how our brain cells live throughout our entire bodies. I wish I had understood about the mind and how to be more mindful and connected with the world inside and outside of us. I wish I had known how to live in such a way that I was always operating from my Highest Potential Self, achieving more success with less stress.

I have since learnt that many of the patterns of thinking, feeling and behaviour I followed in adult life were influenced by my childhood experiences. I was a middle child sandwiched between two brothers, one three years older and one three years younger. As a result of the age and gender differences we didn't tend to play or do things together. I often found solace in books and magazines, mostly about young girls who were strong, confident and capable. My favourite books were the Malory Towers series by Enid Blyton. I could relate to the heroine, Darrell Rivers, who had a bit of a temper which often got her into trouble. Darrell arrived at Malory Towers at the age of twelve, excited and eager to do well. Inspired by Headmistress Miss Grayling's words of welcome, she was determined to be one of Malory Towers' successes. Unfortunately, this didn't come easily to Darrell. The books take you through the ups and downs of a teenager finding her way in life.

I would read these books under my bedcovers with a torch or by the light of the streetlight outside my window. I remember these as very happy times.

My favourite TV characters were The Bionic Woman, Charlie's Angels, Cagney and Lacey and, best of all, Wonder

Woman. All these characters were strong, capable women fighting for justice, yet we would always get to see their more vulnerable side from time to time.

Jamie Sommers was the Bionic Woman, an ex-tennis professional who received super strength and extra capabilities to become a spy.

The characters in Charlie's Angels were Sabrina Duncan, Jill Munroe, and Kelly Garrett, who graduated from the police academy in Los Angeles to become agents for a Private Investigations Agency.

Mary Beth Lacey and Chris Cagney were female police officers in New York City. Cagney was a single, career-minded woman, while Lacey was a married mother. In addition to going after the bad guys, the female leads had to combat sexism in the male-dominated workplace. This is something I had to deal with right from the start in my own career, dealing with disgusting behaviour and comments from my Store Manager when I was just eighteen. At this tender age I hadn't developed any superpowers and didn't have the courage to speak up about my experiences.

Wonder Woman was an Amazonian Princess, from a place and time where beautiful, ageless women with great strength, agility, and intelligence lived. Her alter ego was Diana Prince, a slightly nerdy looking junior officer in the US Navy. Lynda Carter played the Wonder Woman I remember as a young girl. Her character embodied strength, wisdom and compassion. To me she was a role model. A symbol of the extraordinary capabilities that women can have, and I wanted to find mine.

I was tall like Wonder Woman and as a child I had natural dark hair. I wasn't showing any promise of her looks or figure, but I lived in hope I might develop into them. Like Wonder Woman I wanted to stand up for justice. I often felt life at home and at school was unfair and that no one listened to me. At one point I wanted to be a journalist to enable me to seek justice through my work. I fell in love and started a career in management instead, enabling me to earn enough at age eighteen to leave home and buy my first house. The desire for independence from my family home was compelling. I wanted to strike out on my own two feet and become someone in my own right.

Not unlike my childhood heroines, my life has rarely gone to plan. There have been many challenges, some of which I have brought upon myself. In recent years, I have developed my Coaching business (Leaders are Making A Difference) whilst continuing to develop my Highest Potential Self. With all I have learnt I can calmly look back on everything that has gone before with compassion for myself. Rather than regretting anything from my past, I am curious to learn what I can from it, and I have compassion towards those people who made life difficult along the way.

Finally, as a 52-year-old I feel a new sense of ease towards life. I have stopped worrying about what 'might happen' and stopped trying to control everything. I have stopped constantly preparing to defend myself and assuming people are trying to catch me out. I have stopped trying too hard to impress and achieve. This way of being was exhausting!

Instead, I have more realistic expectations of myself and others. I have stopped beating myself up for not being perfect. I have stopped comparing myself to others. I am a work in progress, and I like it that way because I enjoy the process of learning and seeing my progress along the way.

Don't misunderstand me though. I don't want you to think I have taken a step back in success terms. No, this version of me is happier and more successful in all aspects of life than the previous version. I call this version *Super Neuro Me*.

Claire Walton
Coach & Author

TESTIMONIALS

WHAT PEOPLE SAY ABOUT CLAIRE WALTON – MAD
COACH!

Although I have worked with Claire for a relatively short period of time, it is no exaggeration to say Claire has transformed how I approach both challenges and priorities within my role and the pressures we all face as part of normal life.

As CEO of a multi academy trust, my experience was previously steeped in school leadership. Through Claire's breadth of experience and skills as a coach, she has challenged and supported me to be my 'best self' and reflect on how I enable colleagues across the organisation to be their 'best self'.

I find Claire authentic, professional and honest and her expertise in coaching is enabling me to be a curious, confident and courageous leader.

DEBI BAILEY - CEO NEAT ACADEMY TRUST

Working with 'Leaders are MAD' has definitely been a great experience. Claire has a knack for getting to the heart of the matter. Her coaching style is insightful and genuinely uplifting. She has a constructively direct, intuitive approach that really helps teams face the challenges before them and then to navigate an appropriate strategic direction. Claire is flexible in her methods and seeks regular feedback to ensure full engagement....and she is not afraid to change tack if that is the right thing to do.

I have had the pleasure of working with Claire both in a personal capacity as well as part of a senior leadership and executive team. In each case, I have found her to be genuine and appropriately challenging. Definitely not afraid to say it as she sees it but equally set in an agreed framework so that her coaching is received well and not defensively.

In my 121 coaching Claire has helped me to understand others in far more colour, helping me to reflect about my interactions and approach to get the best out of my relationships with others. Claire has also challenged me to take a more determined look at my career choices which has been a real 'eye opening' experience.

The difference Claire has made to me is simply to re-assess my goals and to strive harder in my achievement. She has made me realise where my motivation lies and has helped shine a light on the path to realise that ambition.

BOB ANDREWS – CEO BENENDEN HEALTH

I firmly believe that everyone has a period in their lives where they struggle. For a multitude of reasons, we try to fathom out the, what? Why? When? and how? but often the hardest part can be the 'who?'. For me 'who' related to 'who can I speak to?', 'who will understand?', 'who will help me?' etc. By pure chance, a friend introduced me to Claire, and straight away I'd found my 'who'. All of the other questions that I was struggling to solve on my own were then also answered. She helped me rediscover the person I used to be, and ultimately the person I wanted to be moving forward. For that, I cannot thank her enough. She will always remain affectionately known as 'my Fixer'.

KARL PEMBERTON – MANAGING DIRECTOR –
ACTIVE FINANCIAL PLANNERS

Wow, when it comes to superpowers Claire has them in abundance! Her ability to get right to the real heart of a challenge and work with you to solve it is truly transformational.

I've been working with Claire as a coach for the past three years. We've worked through many different scenarios from transitioning bosses to leaving a role and onwards to securing my dream role and everything in between. Her approach is practical, holistic, and focussed on ensuring you are being truly honest with yourself in all aspects of your life.

Claire's impact on me as a leader and as a mother, wife, sister, friend has been amazing. I'm more confident, collaborative, open, curious and able to embrace life's opportunities. We also have a lot of laughs along the way.

Buy the book, read the book, do the work – it will make a difference. Here's to all our superpowers!"

HELEN SMITH – CHIEF COMMERCIAL OFFICER –
CO-OP LIFE SERVICES

When I first met Claire, I experienced her as a passionate individual with a bubbly personality, full of creativity and great ideas. She has worked with me and my team on a number of occasions. One example was when she co-designed our flagship development programme "Brilliant Conversations". I wanted Claire to help us shake up our approach to Performance Management and get my HR team and our managers to think and behave differently. This programme was a huge success and has helped develop our values led culture. Claire's values are very much aligned to ours and this is of significant importance. She is caring, accountable, commercial and energising. If you also want enthusiasm, leading edge thinking, challenge and innovation then Claire is what you are looking for.

SUSAN FULTON – DIRECTOR OF PEOPLE –
HOME GROUP

Previously my boss, when Head of HR in a Financial Services organisation many years ago, Claire has since continued as one of my mentors, helping me navigate some difficult issues throughout my Career. I have also hired Claire as a Coach for my CEO and other members of the Executive Team, in one of my organisations. As Coach, Claire asks the right questions to get you to see resolutions for yourself. She helps you see the critical issues within the team and identify how you can resolve them effectively. This made a significant difference to our Executive team's effectiveness at a time when we faced many challenges.

What you can expect from Claire is humane, direct professionalism.

ANN CORBYN - EXECUTIVE DIRECTOR, PEOPLE
& ORGANISATIONAL DEVELOPMENT
HERTFORDSHIRE PARTNERSHIP UNIVERSITY
NHS TRUST

I have worked with Claire for many years now. She has supported one of the Exec teams I was part of, helping us to create our organisational strategy and then went on to coach the team to understand how best to work effectively together.

Claire has also coached me for several years and I always find her very knowledgeable, professional and with very high integrity.

ROB PHILLIPS - GROUP FINANCE DIRECTOR THE BBI GROUP

I have known Claire for over ten years. Some descriptions that come to mind are her passion for personal development, tenacity and straight forward approach. Claire has coached many of my aspiring leaders when I worked as a Senior Manager of a large Operations Function. She helped them on their personal and professional transformations and in every case she helped change awareness, motivation and application of skills and behaviour. People weren't just going along with the coaching, they effected real change, for themselves, their teams and the business.

I was also part of a team coached by Claire. Coaching created profound personal and collective discoveries and commitments which we anchored back to for years after.

What Claire does is deliver lasting change at an individual, team and organisational level.

RACHAEL ELLIOTT – COUNSELLOR,
PSYCHOTHERAPIST AND COACH

I met Claire on a one-day authentic leadership course and was instantly drawn to her. As someone in a similar field of work myself, it takes a lot to impress me but Claire really did. Her delivery style, knowledge and clear passion for what she does was inspiring and in just a few short breakout discussions with her, she helped me understand more about my own personal values than I have in my life to date! It was the follow up coaching session though that really made me think 'wow', she is good. Having received coaching on a number of occasions over the years, I had an expectation of how the session would go but I was wrong.

I would describe Claire's approach as eclectic and very client led. She works with what you present to her and has such breadth of knowledge! She very quickly got underneath the surface of some really deep rooted and very personal issues and I can honestly say that one session has been life changing for me, it left me feeling like a ball and chain had been released! Since then, I have commissioned Claire to deliver a couple of work assignments, coaching executives and transforming a very broken team. The feedback has been phenomenal with participants also using the words 'life-changing'. Personally, and in a work capacity I cannot recommend Claire enough, once she connects with you, she is always there for you in whatever capacity you need her and I am now proud to call her my friend.

If I had to describe Claire in one word I'd use phenomenal! If you want to work with an exec coach who will take you to a place you didn't know you were capable of going and who will help you to transform your life, whether that be in a personal sense or at work, Claire is the one for you. She is by a million miles the best coach I have ever had.

LORRAINE MASTERS – DEPUTY DIRECTOR
ORGANISATIONAL DEVELOPMENT
NORTHUMBRIA UNIVERSITY

I have experienced Claire as both a personal coach and delivering sessions on trust with our senior team. Claire provides clarity in her coaching and is able to get you to explore (sometimes uncomfortable) situations. She equips you with tools and techniques to help your situation and encourages testing and refection as part of the process. There are tools I used during and immediately after the coaching and I'm still using those tools years later. Claire has a very open style, is a great listener and has a unique skill in repeating and summarising for you. I have had no hesitation in recommending Claire to my Executive peers and I'm very excited to be able to purchase her new book.

LISA DAVIDSON – CHIEF PEOPLE OFFICER - CONNECT HEATH

Claire has coached and mentored me for many years. For example, she has coached me through an experience of working with a dysfunctional board and in times of conflict with other colleagues. Claire is what I need sometimes as she pushes you, teaches you to look underneath your behaviour and that of others and apply techniques to help you truly understand what is influencing the situation.

She holds a mirror up to you, recommends reading, shares research and sets you homework. Yes homework! She is not pedestrian or mainstream. She is different. Claire works hard on your behalf and expects you to do the same. Whatever the objective you have for coaching she will find a way to help you make the necessary changes to thought patterns and behaviour, changing your outcomes for the better.

Claire is challenging, fun and authentic. The real deal!

HELEN MOLLOY – SENIOR HR LEAD – SOUTH
NORFOLK COUNCIL & BROADLAND DISTRICT
COUNCIL

Claire has been a supporter of My Sisters Place for almost two years and is an ambassador for the charity in supporting our efforts to end violence against women and girls. Claire has supported the charity in many ways: through a series of 'Because you're worth it' workshops delivered for our supporters, coaching for our staff team and fundraising to support our core work.

We were thrilled to work with Claire and were drawn to her company's title recognising that Leaders are Making a Difference and working with leaders across sectors to support this. I have personally attended Claire's workshops and implemented some of the tools and learning into my everyday work and life.

Claire's offer to coach some of our team has been invaluable to those individuals

"Coaching with Claire has helped me to work through everyday challenges, develop my management style and helped me to find solutions. Claire has helped me reflect, see my strengths and focus on my purpose as a leader and motivated me when I have really needed it"

"Claire just gets it. I am so grateful for her input and have had several lightbulb moments after applying her techniques that can be used straightaway"

We would like to congratulate Claire on her first book *Super Neuro You* and say a huge thank you for the ongoing support and time she commits to My Sisters Place.

MICHELLE O'ROURKE - CEO MY SISTER'S PLACE

Journal, Day 1

Twice married and husband number two is already history. I didn't kill him but if he dares to wave and smile at me again like I'm a casual acquaintance then I may have to murder the lying little shit. I cannot believe he had the audacity to acknowledge me so casually, just weeks after being found out as a fraud, thrown out of our house and out of the marriage. Just a mere fifteen weeks after the most perfect wedding ceremony in Santorini. The hope that I had finally met my 'happy ever after' already seems like a lifetime ago.

It is our sixth perfect day in the picturesque village of Imerovigli. It sits at the highest point of the caldera with the very best views of Nea Kameni, Santorini's black volcanic island in the centre of the lagoon.

Earlier this morning, John went for a run whilst I spent an hour in the hotel's outdoor gym, overlooking the beautiful lagoon. Then we ate breakfast on the hotel restaurant terrace, where we drank the first of many glasses of champagne and ate a delicious breakfast of pancakes, bacon and maple syrup and tart fresh berries whilst reading through the wedding cards we had brought with us.

After breakfast we sunbathed and cooled off in the pool. Before going to our rooms to get ready I relaxed further with a full body massage in the hotel spa. I used our suite overlooking the sea to get ready whilst John dressed in a separate room provided by the hotel. A hairdresser and makeup artist came to the room to help me look my best. I wanted everything to be absolutely perfect. My dress was a stunning ivory Italian lace design, very figure hugging in all the right places, with a long train. I had starved myself for the last six months and never failed to hit the gym five days a week to fit into the dress and still be able to breathe. Once dressed and ready to see the complete look, I was very happy with myself.

The ceremony was held at 5 o'clock in the gardens of the hotel overlooking the sea. John cried when he saw me walk into the garden. I cried when I saw him cry. And the tears and laughter continued to flow as we exchanged our vows and read our poems to each other.

We had more laughs taking photos all over the island, posing with locals and chatting in our best, yet still very poor Greek. There was more champagne, more food, and music from the musicians who accompanied us and the photographer everywhere we went.

Now the sun has set and the musicians have left, we settle down for a final round of champagne and even more food. We FaceTime people at home and scroll through all the photos we have taken, laughing at the silly ones and deleting any awful ones.

It is time for bed after an amazing day. I am very, very happy.

I saw him first and was about to dart across the road to avoid him but before I could he looked straight at me. I expected him to hang his head in shame after what he had done. Not this deluded little liar: he waved and smiled with his goofy gap-toothed smile like some ridiculous cartoon character. What the fuck? What planet is he on? I walked on, seething. My blood boiled throughout my entire body. I thought I was going to internally combust. A few seconds later, I turned 180 degrees and walked quickly after him.

I called out, "Hey, Fuckwit, how dare you acknowledge me like some casual acquaintance?" He stopped, turned around and looked at me like an innocent child wondering what on earth he had done wrong.

Without drawing breath, I went on, "You are a pathetic, deluded, deceitful little fuckwit. I know about ALL the lies, ALL the untruths I suspected but allowed you to convince me were real. You're full of shit... you made me think I was going mad. You made me feel guilty for asking so many questions when things didn't add up. You witnessed my frustration and fear and yet continued with all your lies. You married me, vowing to 'openly communicate and protect me from harm'. More fucking lies!"

This was the first time I had told him what I thought of him and his hurtful behaviour and boy, did it feel good! He stood there, facing me, toe to toe and looking like a rabbit in the headlights. He wasn't expecting this.

What did he think I was going to do? After that awful day, just two weeks ago, when he finally admitted to lying to me for the past five years. He had lied about his jobs and income. He even admitted fabricating client invoices in his attempt to cover his lies to me. This was all after he had put us in financial jeopardy by losing his job after ignoring all the signs and my advice.

Worst of all, when I asked him why he lied, he blamed me. He said he thought I would think he wasn't good enough for me, so he had to pretend to be more than he was. He didn't know me at all. As if I could care less how much he earned. Honesty and intelligence and good character, this is what I cared about. I thought this was him.

I waited for him to respond but as always with him, he just stood there saying nothing. He didn't reply. He didn't try to defend his behaviour and the lies. I said, "You can't say anything, can you, because all you would say is more lies. You are not worth any more of my time or energy." I stood still, in silence, waiting for him to say something, anything, and after the longest minute of my life, still absolutely nothing. Feeling angry and frustrated, I turned another 180 degrees and walked in the direction of home.

I need to draw a line under the past five years and start the next chapter of my life, but it's hard to do this when I am still married to him and can't divorce him until we've been married a year. The red mist left me, and my heart rate slowed. I wondered if shouting at him had made me feel any better. No, it hadn't. It felt absolutely bloody fantastic when I was shouting, but now I just felt like I had given him the upper hand. I can hear him now, talking to people, saying I'm the nutcase, not him.

To cheer myself up I called Abi and invited her to join me for a week in the sun. I couldn't really afford it but what the hell, I needed a holiday! Abi said yes to a free holiday, of course, and within a few weeks we were lying by the pool, drinking Prosecco in the sun. Time away with my favourite person in the whole world and a chance to absorb exactly what had happened over the last few months was exactly what I needed.

Abi and I have always been close. I'm not sure if that's because it's been just us since I left her dad when she was five or if we would always have been like this. She's not as outwardly confident as me; she's quieter and more considered. I wish I could be more like her sometimes. I think as we get older, she is becoming more like me and I am becoming more like her. We seem to be learning from the best bits of each other.

We look alike too. Two blondes with blue eyes and big smiles. Abi is a few inches shorter and more of an hourglass than my leggier slightly pear-shaped frame, but we can still share some of the same clothes and we are the same shoe size, which is very handy.

Since moving from London Abi has lost her southern accent and taken on a posh Leeds twang which suits her. I am so proud of her. She is working for a charity helping vulnerable young women get out of their difficult circumstances and achieve successful lives. It doesn't pay well even though she is already in a management role, and I support her financially every now and again as I want her to continue to work in a role supporting such an important cause.

Journal, Day 30

It's the last night of our holiday. Earlier, Abi came onto the terrace, sat on the sofa next to me, wrapped her arm in mine and lay her head on my shoulder. Her tenderness made me feel so soothed and content, reminding me of when she was a baby lying in my arms. I asked her what she thought I should do to help me move forward. I trust her insight and judgement. She has a wise head on young shoulders, and she knows me better than anyone. She told me, "Mum just do what you always do: move forward, be positive and do what makes you happy. You could spend time dwelling on the past and when you eventually move on and look back you will think, "Well, what a waste of time that was." This was good advice.

It's only a few more years until I will be fifty and time is running out to make sure I have my 'shit' – and by 'shit' I mean my life – worked out by then.

Tonight, on the terrace, I vowed to take Abi's advice and just get on with being happy. I have decided that by the time I am fifty I will make sure life is 'Fabulous'.

Journal, Day 31

First day back from the holiday and I am sick. I planned to make a start on becoming 'fabulous by 50' by getting up early, doing an hour of Pilates and taking Abi for a healthy breakfast. I tried Pilates but my head thumped every time I put it down. The healthy breakfast went out of the window as I gave in to a bacon buttie smothered in ketchup. Not a good start to a healthier, fitter, slimmer me. Abi also wants to lose weight and get fitter. This will give me an extra incentive to be good. I need to be a role model for her. I have tried to be a role model for Abi all her life. It's been my number one goal and yet I often feel I am letting her down.

After Abi left to go back to her house on the other side of Leeds, I felt unexpectedly sad. I had loved having her company for the week and now I was back on my own again I felt lonelier than I had before the holiday. I think in the last few weeks I have been on automatic pilot, not connecting emotionally with anything. Time with Abi brought positive emotions flooding back but without her here I was soon drowning in sadness, disbelief and despair for the first time in months.

After indulging in a pity party for half an hour I acknowl-edged such pathetic behaviour was not helpful and resolved to drive to Tesco for fruit and vegetables. I wanted to treat myself but after considering chocolate and cake and, worst of all, wine, I decided none of these would be helpful in my quest for fabulousness. Instead, I treated myself to a fillet steak and spinach. I made four green smoothies with cucumber, celery, broccoli, lime, apple, pineapple, spinach and avocado, and ginger shots for the next few days. I drank a smoothie for supper, but I still didn't feel fabulous. My cold lingered on my chest and I had a raging headache.

The rest of the day was spent on the sofa, getting up and down every now and again for a cup of tea and sorting out the washing. I was also on Facebook which I think is good for me and bad for me in equal measure. I find it a good support when feeling on my own as the contact with others, albeit virtual, fills a need inside me. On the other hand, seeing people with their boyfriends, husbands and family reminds me of the fact that I'm here spending most of Sunday on my own again. At least I had Poldark to look forward to at 9pm. I love watching broody and handsome Poldark. He is so strong, fit and sexy. But I could not believe the ending. He cheats on Demelsa with stuck up and pathetic Elizabeth. FFS, Demelsa is a hundred times the woman Elizabeth is. I decide I hate men and go to bed. Achieving 'Fabulous' isn't going to be easy. I need sleep.

Journal, Day 32

I started my day with a lemon and hot water drink to cleanse my system. I was very impressed with myself. I drank one of my green juices for a late breakfast and the day was off to a good start. My brother called to ask how I was, and I got a bit upset. I don't know exactly why. He wasn't prepared for this. He clearly felt awkward and suggested we meet for coffee in the afternoon. He probably hoped I would be past tears by then and he was right. We had a good old moan about life, and I felt better for it. At the end of the call Mark said, "Cheer up sis, you will be fine. You've got enough of us that love you, don't go spilling any more tears over that waste of space."

I replied with a half-smile, trying to put my brave face back on again. But when I put the phone down, I still felt down and lonely. I focused on the fact I have a pretty good life regardless of its challenges and I have my brother, who is a decent man, even if he is also a pain sometimes. He proves that decent, honest men exist somewhere out there, giving me hope. I picked the phone up again and called Bridget. Bridget has been seeing a coach recently and she swears this woman has changed her life.

I've tried coaching before through work and had some benefit but nothing particularly transformational. They have tended to be a good source of a second perspective on my issues and have helped me to reframe situations and think through how best to tackle challenges. I've never found anyone who ever got to the real core issues that hold me back and stop me from being the very best version of me though. If I am to have this fabulous version of me by the time I am fifty then I need someone to help me understand what it is that needs to change for me to make a real difference in my life.

Apparently, this woman calls herself a MAD coach because what she does is help people Make A Difference in the world, starting with themselves. I often feel like I am going

MAD these days. I am certainly very mad at John and when I think about it, I have been mad at a lot of people. I think I have a lot of pent-up anger in me. I have had for a long time. After the call with Bridget, I sent an email to this MAD Coach and asked for an online meeting to see if I like her and if she can help me.

Journal, Day 33

I set the alarm with enough time for at least half an hour of Pilates before my first Zoom call with my team at 8.00 am, but I pressed the snooze button three times before getting up.

I had woken up from a horrible dream in which I was with ex-husband number one and he had taken Abi from me and disappeared off to Japan, of all places. With the trauma of the dream ending like this I wanted to go back to sleep to dream up a nicer ending. I couldn't go back to sleep after three attempts and ran out of time and had to get up. So annoying. I pulled myself together just in time for my call.

During the call I was distracted from one of the presenta-tions made by Janet. I had started ruminating. What did the dream mean? Am I worried I am going to lose Abi to her Dad? Is it fundamentally a fear of being totally on my own? Abi is my constant. Men may come and go but Abi is always there for me to love and be loved by. I worry this might make my relationship with her unhealthy. Do I need her more than she needs me now? Does she feel this? Is this a pressure for her? I was starting to get a headache from all the overthinking. Thankfully, Janet didn't seem to notice I was distracted.

I am meeting the MAD Coach tomorrow. We have an online meeting arranged after work. I'm working from home again so that I can finish at five and have the call with her at half past. I'm not sure what to expect. Bridget has given her a great testimonial. I've looked at her website and she intrigues me. She seems to have a fascination with superheroes. I've always loved Wonder Woman. Perhaps she can bring the Wonder Woman out in me.

Journal, Day 34 - Meeting the Coach

The meeting is online, which makes sense as it's just a chemistry meeting and we may not get on. Claire greets me from her desk in what appears to be a home office set up. She is dressed smart casual, wearing a pale pink jumper and silver necklace and earrings. She looks relaxed, confi-dent, warm and smiley. I like her immediately. After the usual introductions and chat about the weather we soon get to discussing my reasons for the video call.

I say, "I have had coaching before through work. It's been a while though... I'm currently The Chief Commercial Officer at Health Foods. I've worked there for the past five years. I love my job and the organisation. I have a great team and one of the best CEOs I have ever worked for. I feel so lucky to be able to say this as it hasn't always been the case. It's not perfect, but then nothing is."

I see Claire making notes as I speak. I'm intrigued about what she might be writing, but I carry on telling her about myself. "On the downside," I say, "I work very long hours and travel a lot. There are lots of overnight stays, with lots of eating out and eating the wrong things. It's hard to stick to healthy habits, which is ironic since we are a health-based company. It can be quite hard trying to be everything for everyone. But I love feeling needed and valued and an integral part of the team, so I guess it's worth all the stress that comes with it."

I pause. Claire asks, "So, Laura, are you saying you want help sticking to some healthier habits?"

I hadn't thought about it specifically until just now but find myself replying, "Yes, I would. I need to look after myself more. I'm not getting any younger and I don't want to feel frumpy and fifty."

Claire moves towards the screen slightly and asks, "And when you say it's hard being everything for everyone, would you like it to be less hard for you?"

I think about her question for a while and reply, "I suppose so... I hadn't thought about it quite that clearly until I said it out loud. I do find it hard, tiring, annoying and sometimes it makes me angry that I do so much for others, and I wonder who is caring about me and what I need?"

"Okay, Laura, we can work on these things together. If you hadn't thought of these specifics before, what was it that brought you to me?"

I start to feel a bit in the spotlight all of a sudden, a bit exposed. I pick up my coffee and hold it in front of me with both my hands. The warmth of the cup feels reassuring.

"I haven't seen a coach for a while. Work has been going so well, I didn't feel I needed anyone to support me... It's actually more a challenge I have had in my personal life that brings me to you. I heard from my friend Bridget that you help people to stop getting in the way of themselves and I want this for me. I feel like I am somehow making my life harder than it needs to be. I am angry and frustrated a lot of the time but don't know what to do to change how I am feeling. I've recently separated from my husband and I am very angry towards him... and myself for enabling him to manipulate me. I just want to move on past the anger but don't seem to be able to."

Claire is waiting for me to continue. I say, "To be honest, it's not just about him. I feel like I have been living my whole life limited by something in me and my recent situation with 'Fuckwit', as I have taken to calling him, has just brought it all to a head. I am going to be fifty in a few years, and I don't want to feel like this about myself for the next four or five decades. I worry that perhaps I am at an age where I am who I am, and I just need to accept myself, good and bad. After all, I am successful in many ways. I have a very well-paid job, I have a wonderful grown-up daughter, I have friends and I'm relatively fit and healthy."

There is something about the warmth and openness in the way Claire looks at me that keeps me talking and I share much more than I expected to. She seems totally relaxed, and yet laser focused on me and every word I say. I feel like she even knows the thoughts I have that I'm not sharing.

When Claire speaks next, she describes the basis of her work. She says, "Whilst I use the shorthand label of 'Coaching', I tend to provide a mixture of coaching, mentoring and some therapy inspired approaches. I must be clear that I am not a qualified therapist or psychologist. I have, however, been trained to use a number of therapeutic techniques within my toolkit and I have studied a number of aspects of psychology and neuroscience. I use this throughout my work."

That's fine by me. I'm not looking for a therapist. I remember, when things fell apart during the weeks after the wedding, I saw a therapist. In the sessions, all I did was listen to him justify his credibility. He constantly spoke about himself and his other clients and how he helped them. In the four hours and £200 I wasted with him I hardly opened my mouth. When I did say something, he told me I had hurt his feelings. Apparently, I had said, "People who wallow constantly in their own self-pity are pathetic and I don't want to be pathetic. That's not how I see myself." I was expressing myself openly, without the fear of judgement.

He told me he was hurt because my comment was made just after he had described how he had become a Therapist after receiving counselling and my comment suggested I saw him as pathetic. WTF! The main reason I wanted to see him was to have someone to talk to without worrying about their feelings and the impact anything I might say would have on them. I hope Claire isn't going to get all sensitive with me if I just speak my mind. Thankfully, she already seems completely different to him; much more objective whilst also being empathetic.

Claire seems to notice I am thinking and not totally present. She asks if I'm okay and I share my story of the overly sensitive therapist. She tells me she understands my concerns and reassures me her focus is always on me and that she has her own coaching supervision to make sure she doesn't get sensitive to anything I might bring up.

She goes on to say, "It is often a misconception that coaching is needed when there is a problem to solve. My approach is much less about solving a problem and much more about helping you be your Highest Potential Self. Whilst I don't brand myself as a 'Life Coach' my work has at its heart the entire life of the client. I take a fully integrated approach. Professional and personal, the past, the present and the future. Often people are struggling because they aren't integrated in their brains, bodies and therefore in their minds, as well as inside and outside of their work roles. If we work together, I will explain more about this.

"You're not on your own thinking you may be too hardwired into the who you have been for many years and that fundamental change is going to be difficult or even impossible, but this is simply not the case. Some of the main reasons people don't change are because they don't know how, they don't want to put the work into making the changes stick or they are scared of what they might have to let go of as part of that change. Does any of this resonate for you?"

It does, it totally resonates. If I knew how to change, I would have made those changes years ago. I tell Claire, "I want to live my whole life in a more effective way because, whilst I've achieved relative success, I don't feel it and I am sad that I don't feel successful."

She asks, "What do you feel then Laura?"

"I feel exhausted, wrung out, empty."

Claire gives a knowing smile and her head tilts slightly to the right. "I understand. I've been there. I often think, I wish my younger self (an Executive Director and single mum) knew what I know now. I could have saved myself so much stress emotionally and physically. I could have been more successful than I was and felt happier at the same time with far fewer dramas. My life works for me on every level now I know what I know, and I practise what I know. Practise is crucial, and eventually things become second nature. Would you like me to share a little more about the neuroscience bit?"

I am ready to learn all she has to share. She seems so 'altogether', 'very happy in her own skin', not perfect... she has clearly been through some stuff of her own and is through the other side. I respect her for that and I'm grateful to her for sharing with me.

She explains, "Before I start sharing, I want you to know that today will be the most talking I am likely to do in our sessions. Once you understand the principles of the approach we will take together, most of the talking will be down to you. I'm here to help you understand yourself and to become the best version of you. I will share some techniques with you and some exercises you can do outside the sessions, but it will definitely be you who does the work."

I tell Claire that I'm good with this. I like her no nonsense style. I am prepared to do the work if it makes a difference.

Claire starts to tell me about the neuroscience she uses in her approach. "One of the fundamental teachings of neuro-science is neuroplasticity of the brain. Have you heard of this?" she says.

I think I have, but I don't know all about it. I ask Claire to explain.

"Our brain enables new patterns of connections between neurons to be created. Let's call them pathways. Coaching is one of the best ways to help a person create a change in outcomes by identifying their unhelpful pathways and swap them for new, more helpful ones. It is much harder to make these changes on your own.

"Over time our well-practised thought processes and behaviours have created default pathways in our brains. The more we use a neural pathway, the more developed it becomes. This is great when learning a new skill or helpful habit like when learning to drive, for example. Every time you practice, 'Mirror, signal, manoeuvre,' you strengthen the pathway for that pattern of activity until, with practise, this becomes automatic. But it is this sort of neural patterning that also keeps us stuck in an unhelpful habit or way of working."

Claire gives me another example. "Let's say a client has a well-worn neural pathway for putting the needs of others first (most likely based on a deep need to be loved and a fear of not being loved). It is going to be a tough pattern to shift, but not impossible. Does this make sense to you?"

It does make sense. I am feeling hopeful as she explains. Hope that with her help I can change for the better. I can feel a tingling sensation at the back of my neck. "Absolutely," I say. "I think this example may actually be one of my unhelpful patterns of behaviour. I'm exhausted by constantly looking after the needs of others and being the responsible one and it's getting me down."

I encourage Claire to tell me more.

She says, "I can help you form new neural pathways. We'll be using strategies such as: asking you to envision a different future; digging deep into why you have developed the patterns you have; encouraging you to look directly at issues rather than avoiding them, then building new patterns. Some of the techniques may feel very conceptual, some practical; some might feel odd, even silly, but all will be based upon well-researched and effective psychological and neuroscientific principles. How does that sound to you?"

It sounds quite different to the coaching I have had in the past, and I say so. Most of that was more skills based, such as influencing skills or communication skills. It's weird - Claire seems to hear my inner thoughts.

She says, "Everything we do together will enhance your ability to apply all the leadership skills you already have, because we will work on how you can always bring your Highest Potential Self to whatever you are doing. Like I said before, working together you can become a better leader at work and have a healthier and happier way of life."

This is absolutely what I want. Claire says she can be an Accountability Partner to increase my motivation to practise what I learn and a Reflection Partner helping me to review the practice and the new outcomes I achieve. This all sounds exactly what I need.

"I can help you identify opportunities for tweaking the approaches you practise and offer you more techniques to ensure sustainable success," she offers. "Do you have any questions for me at this stage, Laura?"

"A couple," I said. "You said I might find some of the techniques you use silly or odd. What sort of thing were you talking about there?"

"Good question. As I said before, whilst I brand myself as an Executive and Leadership Coach, I take an integrated approach. Most people and most people's lives tend not to be fully integrated and yet our best performance as well as positive wellbeing is achieved when we live and work as fully integrated beings."

"Sorry, Claire," I said. "I'm not sure I understand what you mean. I sort of get it, but could you expand?"

"Of course. I help clients integrate the many aspects of who they are, which makes them much more effective and happier. For example, some clients think they should leave emotion out of their decision making and yet all decisions are driven by emotion. We need to understand the emotional elements of our thinking as much as the rational elements. Understanding how emotions are created and how to manage them to create better outcomes is a key part of my coaching approach."

"Through neuroscience we are learning that to be fully effective we need to accept the integration of the brain and body and work with this. Did you know 80% of the time our body is telling our brain what to do rather than the other way around?"

I didn't know that. I always assumed our brain told our body what to do. I tell Claire this. I also tell her I am fascinated by the science and would like to learn more.

She continues, "This is one of the reasons we need to understand how our body is feeling and what we are doing with our body that is helping to generate that feeling. To access less conscious, more emotional, parts I often use approaches such as metaphor and people sometimes find this odd. When I encourage them to focus on body sensations connected with their thinking or to stand, sit or move in a particular way to generate new thinking they can sometimes find they feel silly."

Claire asks me if I will be happy trying new things even if they feel odd or silly, now that I understand the science behind it.

"I think so. I guess I will have to see, but I'm glad I asked."

I notice I am no longer feeling as exposed and vulnerable as I was when I initially started opening up to Claire. I am feeling more and more confident Claire is the right coach for me as she clearly knows her stuff. I can tell a bullshitter a mile off, or at least I thought I could before 'Fuckwit'.

Claire says, "People are often uncomfortable being asked to do things they don't fully understand and can often perceive these situations as slightly threatening. Learning requires us to be open to trying new things and it is amazing how this can make people feel unsafe. We humans are highly programmed to want certainty: we hate ambiguity. We are programmed to be ready to react to potential threat, and uncertainty and ambiguity threaten us.

"Have you heard how we are pre-programmed for fight ,flight, freeze and appease?"

I have but I'm fascinated and ask Claire to explain it to me.

"Our reptilian brain, also known as the limbic system, was the earliest part of the brain to develop. It's been helping us to survive for a hundred million years, and it continues to do so. When our survival instinct kicks in, our brains and bodies are pumped with adrenalin and cortisol which are designed to have us think less and react instead.

"You are probably familiar with the example of a sabre-tooth tiger coming at you. In this situation you don't want to think through your options from a variety of perspectives, you want your feet to move quickly, and you want to be stronger and faster than usual. To promote these physical responses your brain floods your body with cortisol and adrenalin and afterwards we are exhausted from an excess of these neurochemicals.

"So fast forward to 2021. There are no sabre-tooth tigers, just a never-ending supply of emails, constant notifications pinging, relentless video meetings, high expectations and a long list of people who need you to do something for them. Does any of this ring a bell?"

"It certainly does. I don't think I've ever been so distracted trying to manage the constant interruptions of technology alongside the sheer volume and complexity of my work."

Claire continues, "The result is that our limbic systems are pumped up with these chemicals when we don't need them to be, and in this state, we aren't able to really think, create, or choose effectively. You have mentioned being exhausted a few times in our conversation today. This may be a response to too much cortisol and adrenalin in your system."

Listening to Claire explain the threat response, I can see how I have lived a lot of my life feeling under constant threat. Not necessarily always significant threat or even actual threat but constant perceived threat, small real threats and some huge real threat. If I could learn to manage my reactions more effectively and as a result have more energy that would be amazing. I feel like I should be taking notes, there is so much to learn. I will make notes when we have the proper sessions. I've already decided I'm going ahead with this.

I say, "I can completely relate to this, Claire. When you explain this, it makes complete sense as to why I am always so tired and with events over the past few months I'm surprised I've managed to stay awake and function."

"Bless you, Laura. I know the feeling. I've been there myself. I know what it is like to be running on cortisol and adrenalin and not finding the time to boost your oxytocin and serotonin. Like you, I had an Executive career before coaching. I understand the high expectations of the role, the constant demand on your time and energy and the difficulty of doing this and being a mum, partner, daughter and friend. I've been there. It can be tough if you don't know how best to navigate it."

Claire adds, "We women, in particular, think we should be able to do it all and without complaining or asking for support. Am I right?"

"Yes, this is exactly how it feels. Over the years I've tried so hard to be this role model woman and I just feel like I keep failing. I'm exhausted. I have constant aches and pain. My shoulders are stiff as can be and I have frequent headaches and Irritable Bowel Syndrome. Do you think this is linked?"

"Most likely, yes."

"If I change how I navigate all I have on my plate, do you think I could stop the tiredness, the aches and pains and feel energetic and healthy again?"

"I do, these things are generally all linked. It's part of the integration I spoke about. The right sort of coaching can definitely help clients change the way they feel, literally! I can help you learn how to move more of your brain activity out of your limbic system and into the prefrontal cortex or 'executive brain'.

Claire continues, "The high trust relationship we develop in our coaching sessions releases oxytocin which dilutes the effect of cortisol. If you are prepared to be open minded and give things a go, you will learn to move out of automatic limbic reaction and into more conscious choice and engagement of your executive brain. When this happens, you will release gaba, which calms your nervous system, creating a feel-good effect. What you learn in our sessions, you practise outside the sessions, generating more success and better mental and physical health. With practise, your responses to day-to-day pressures will be more appropriate for the actual threat or you will perceive no threat at all."

It all sounded a bit too good to be true and I find myself saying this to Claire.

She answers, "I know. I used to think that before I knew what I know now and before I started putting it into practice for myself. I can share lots of testimonials of people who came to coaching with similar goals to you and they have experienced huge shifts in performance and wellbeing. In the meantime, you said you had a couple of questions?"

I have lots more questions, but I am conscious the chemistry session is a freebie, and I don't want to seem like I am taking advantage of Claire's generosity with her time. But there is one thing that I have wanted to ask her ever since looking at her website.

"This might sound like a daft question... where does your superhero branding come from? What's the story behind it? I used to love Wonder Woman when I was growing up in the seventies and one of the characters on your website looks a bit like Wonder Woman."

She rocks back in her chair and laughs. She has been both professional and warm until now. Now she seems to come to life so much more. She beams across at me and tells me about her childhood aspiration to be like Wonder Woman.

"Did you know the TV series was based on the comic book *Wonder Woman?*" she asks.

I didn't. I just assumed she started in the TV series. Claire soon puts me right.

"Wonder Woman first appeared in All Star Comics in the forties. She is a founding member of the Justice League. I love those films."

She asks me if I have seen the Wonder Woman film that came out in 2017. I haven't. She tells me I must watch it.

"Her new look is fantastic, and it shares more of her back story and a more holistic view of her character and values emerges. I loved it. I have always loved the superhero concept. I love this central principle of them doing the right thing, having superpowers, but also being flawed and having weakness such as Superman and his Kryptonite. I also love the fact that they tend not to be as successful on their own. They are better together as the Justice League. And even Batman had Alfred and later his sidekick, Robin. It proves we all need people, even superheroes. I like to think of myself as a bit of an Alfred to my superhero clients."

I laugh at the comparison. Claire is much younger than Alfred. I'd say she is in her late 40s. She is vibrant... full of energy for life and, well, Alfred is an old man, a bit wrinkly, pale and stoic. I tell her I can't see the physical similarities, but I always liked Alfred, particularly the Michael Caine version. He's a good calming influence and helps Bruce Wayne whenever he comes home from a night of being a superhero. He's always there, ready to patch him up and offer a pep talk. I could do with an Alfred!

"Yes, something like that," Claire says. "Alfred always has Batman's needs and wants as his focus whilst applying some of his curiosity and compassion, creativity, clarity and calm to challenge and support Batman in equal measure. He is also 100% confidential, keeping all Batman's and Bruce Wayne's secrets. These are some of the qualities I like to think I have and less so the stoic old man persona. To be honest, I just love a bit of playfulness in my work. I used to be way too serious when I was an Exec Director. Now I do my own thing I am far more confident expressing myself with humour and playfulness. It's also good to do this to generate more creative thinking."

I can relate to that. I definitely want to have more fun in my work and life. I often feel I'm living in my head too much, overthinking things and constantly worrying about doing the right thing. I know some people think I'm a little too intense. I wish I could let go of whatever it is that makes me feel this constant need to present myself as being on top of everything.

I also tell her, "You said earlier about integration. I compartmentalise work and play but to the point where I think I don't play anymore. It's like 'work hard' is in this huge box and 'play and have fun and relax' is in this tiny little box which, the more I think about it, I hardly ever open. God, no wonder I've been feeling so resentful of people who have the balance right."

At the end of the session, which I don't want to be over, Claire summarises my coaching goals as:

- Manage my emotional reactions to be more appropriate to people and situations and create a healthier and happier me.
- Consider my needs and make them more of a priority, including following healthier habits.
- Stop overthinking things.
- Achieve more for less stress.
- Feel energised, not exhausted and wrung out.
- Feel successful and happy about my success.

We will probably identify more as we work together but these are definitely enough to be getting on with. We agree I should budget for us to work together over the next twelve months and for a session a month. If coaching can help me achieve all of this, it will be worth every penny. I can't wait to get started.

Journal - Day 47

I still have this cold on my chest. I'm sort of ignoring it – well, until I just mentioned it. God willing, it will be gone by the weekend. Here's hoping for better dreams tonight.

Last night I went to sleep trying to dream about Gerard Butler, bare-chested, hair ruffled and covered in sweat! Sadly, I did not dream about Gerard Butler, in any state of dress or undress. In fact, I cannot remember dreaming at all, which I think is a good thing, a sign my mind is fairly at rest. After all, it should be easier to sleep now I don't have hundreds of unanswered questions running around my brain, trying to work out how I can get to the bottom of husband number two's bullshit and lies.

I can't wait for my session with Claire later today. We are going to meet in person for my first session at a really nice hotel in York. I've used this hotel before for meetings and the lounge area is gorgeous, so relaxing and quite spacious for us to have a private conversation. I'm already looking forward to having a good few hours to get things out and start the process of becoming a better version of myself.

I've been reading some background on neuroscience. Claire recommended some books on her website. I started with an easy one;

The Idiot Brain: A Neuroscientist Explains What Your Head is Really Up To.

(BURNETT, 2017)

I've already started noticing how I am thinking more and catching myself thinking unhelpful thoughts, but I can't move away from those unhelpful thoughts. It's fascinating stuff, I'm wondering why this sort of thing is not a fundamental part of Leadership Development. I think I will talk to our Learning and Development team to ask if we can look into this.

Whilst I've made time for reading this book, I haven't found the time to address my poor habits. Ah, well, one step at a time. Let's see just how MAD this MAD coach is and whether she can Make A Difference with me.

The First Coaching Session

I arrive at the hotel a few minutes early for my session and Claire is already there. She has secured us a corner table, making it nice and private for a confidential conversation. It also benefits from the lovely sunlight coming through the window. Claire stands up and waves me over.

As I reach the table she holds out her hand to greet me. She holds my hand for longer than I'm used to, and it was nice, reassuring, comforting. She looks me in the eye, and says, "I'm so looking forward to working with you today."

Claire orders lattes for us and two glasses of water. Once again she radiates warmth, smiling and laughing as we exchange a bit about our day so far. I immediately feel settled and primed to open up and learn.

Claire explains that today's session is going to focus on an exercise designed to get me into a positive emotional state in which I will imagine my ideal future, a future when I am living my Highest Potential Self (HPS). It sounds great but I am worried. I say, "This sounds great, although I don't have a very good imagination. I hope I'm going to be good enough for you."

"Laura, you will be brilliant," Claire says. "Sometimes we just need a little help to do things well that we normally find tricky. That's what I'm here for. Remember, I'm your Alfred and I have your back."

I relax back a little more in my chair and trust myself to be safe in Claire's capable hands. She seems so confident that I also feel confident.

Claire says, "Remember what I said about being playful and having fun as a way to help creativity. Well, to help you access your imagination I want you to be relaxed, move away from that self-critical perspective and be open to possibilities. To do this we are going to start with a mindfulness exercise. Are you up for that?"

This is great, I tell Claire. I keep reading about how useful mindfulness is but never have the time to try it.

A Grounding Exercise to enable presence and support creative thinking

[1]I invite you to find a position which is comfortable for you and at the same time maintains your attention. Check that your shoulders have dropped and plant your feet on the ground.

Now gently close your eyes, and for the next few breaths bring your full focus of attention to your breathing. During these breaths, notice the feeling of the air flowing in through the nostrils, down into the lungs, and down into the belly as you inhale... and on the exhale, feel the release of any tension as you let the air out slowly.

Wonderful. Now I invite you to listen to the sounds you can hear; listen without effort, just allow the sounds around you to be noticed by you.

Notice them and enjoy them for their sound.

Do not try to interpret them or allow them to irritate, just notice.

Allow your range of listening to go beyond the immediate space around you and allow in the sounds from a distance, perhaps from outside this room. Just listen and notice and enjoy the sound for its sound and for nothing else.

I invite you now to allow your mind to open up to what you can smell. Notice what you smell close to you.

Take a deep breath and allow your nose to fill with whatever smells are immediately brought to your attention.

Take another deep breath and see what smells from further afar waft in under your nose, and take another breath to allow these smells to fill your nose as you breathe naturally, enjoying the smells that flow around you and inside you.

If your mind wanders just gently bring it back to your sense of what you can smell.

Staying with your eyes closed, notice what you taste in your mouth.

Notice what you can taste on the tip of your tongue (pause), in the middle of your tongue (pause), at the back of your mouth (pause), down the sides of your cheeks. If your mind wanders just gently bring it back to your sense of what you can taste.

Moving to what you can feel pressing against your body, I invite you to feel your feet on the floor.

Notice the sensation of your feet against your shoes.

Notice the feelings in your left foot and right foot, your left toes and right toes, your left heel and right heel, your left arch and right arch. If your mind wanders just gently bring it back to your sense of what you can feel.

And in a moment, without speaking or changing your posture, I will invite you to open your eyes and notice what you can see: the colours, the shapes, the lightness, the darkness.

Allow your eyes to look left (pause), look right (pause), look up (pause), look down.

If your mind wanders just gently bring it back to your sense of what you can see. Take it all in without questioning or critiquing, without judgement or translation.

You might like to take another few seconds to sit quietly, holding on to this sense of presence and spaciousness from thinking.

This is fab. As Claire guides me through the exercise I feel as though my senses come to life and my body is more alive than normal. My brain is more focused. I feel very present despite the distractions around me and the many balls I was previously juggling in my head. When we are finished the exercise, Claire asks me how I am feeling.

I say, "Wow, I feel so open and light. I don't know how to express it. It probably sounds daft, but I feel so much bigger than I am, almost expanded, taking up more space in the room and It's like I'm breathing from every pore rather than just from my nose and mouth. Is that normal?"

She seems pleased with my response and confirms this is a normal response. I am ready to let my creative juices flow and start the focus for the session. Claire makes detailed notes of all of my responses. She says she will email her notes to me after the session. I sit back and relax.

[2]Claire says, "Now I invite you to close your eyes and imagine walking forward through time to a point in the future when you feel you are achieving all that you wish for. In this place you are successful in all aspects of life and you feel successful. When you get to this place, say, 'I am here now.'"

"I am here, now, I think."

"Laura, what do you see in this place?"

"I see me floating through my office effortlessly looking all smiley and happy. People are smiling back at me and the atmosphere all around me is one of light and joy and colour. People look happy and animated. Most people seem to be in conversation with others, huddled at desks and at whiteboards. I get a sense there is lots of creativity and collaboration going on."

"Laura, what can you hear going on around you?" Claire asks.

I say, "I hear laughter and excitable voices. I hear people asking questions in an interested rather than challenging way. I hear a general buzz but it's not so noisy I can't concentrate. I feel like I am slightly above the noise. The noise is positive and it's fuelling me with positive energy rather than being a distraction. A team member is calling me over to join a group at the whiteboard and asking for my input. I feel like I'm part of the team, the conversation, the buzz and yet able to see and hear everything with clarity rather like being in slow motion."

"What other feelings do you notice?"

"There's a warmth in and around my torso; it feels like it might be pride. Yes, it's like pride keeping me warm."

"What do you sense is creating this feeling?"

"I want to say I feel pride in the team and the organisation and myself. It feels a bit embarrassing admitting to feeling pride in myself, but this feels true to me and I feel it needs to be said out loud."

"It sounds like you are switching from sometimes seeing yourself in the scene and at other times being within the body of your future self. Is this right?" Claire asks.

"Yes, I started seeing myself floating through the office and now it is more like I am there, I am in the body of my future self."

"Can you imagine yourself leaving the office and going home? What are you seeing now?"

"I am getting out of my car, which is an oyster-coloured sports car with the roof down. It's a sunny day and I'm walking towards a modern looking house, not my current house. It is by the beach, literally at the edge of the beach. There is another car, a 4x4 on the driveway, with racks on the roof for surf boards and bikes."

"I am walking through the house, which is open plan and modern, and yet beach style cosy, with lots of pastel colours and different textures, not cluttered but warm and welcoming. It's clearly not a house with children in it so no grandchildren yet."

"I can see a man stood on the deck looking towards the sea. He is tall, and wide across the shoulders, slim but not too slim, dressed in dark blue shorts and a pale blue crumpled shirt. There is a salad prepared on the table on the deck, and two places are set with two wine glasses and a bottle of white wine chilling."

"Wow this is amazing detail, Laura, well done. Are you able to hear, smell or taste anything?"

"Yes, I can hear the waves crashing on the beach and seagulls or something. I can also hear some music playing quietly on a record player in the corner of the living area. It's playing that song 'Summer Breeze' by Seals and Croft. It all feels so chilled and easy and natural. I can taste the freshness of the air and imagine tasting the wine crisp and cold against the warmth of the day. I am walking barefoot on warm, white, wooden floorboards. I notice there is a little sand on the floor as I venture onto the deck. When I walk outside the gentle sea breeze cools me instantly and in a way that is comforting on my skin. I feel really emotional sharing this with you."

"How would you describe that emotion, Laura?"

"It's like my heart is coming out of my chest with a mixture of excitement and happiness and at the same time I feel a little fuzzy headed all of a sudden as if I am telling myself this is just a dream."

"Okay, Laura, I understand. Keep your eyes closed and uncross your legs, feet comfortably flat on the ground. I want you to imagine taking your seat on the deck and getting comfortable in it, feet comfortably on the ground. How does that feel?"

"That feels better; I feel more grounded here. I am looking out to sea and I hear all the noises and see all the colours of the sea and the sand, and then I can feel the cold glass of wine in my hand and the softness of the cushion on my seat and now the man, who I can't fully see, has hold of my hand in his. His hand is warm, dry, a little worn, very comforting. It feels very natural."

"Laura, your imagination is fantastic. Stay with it and really take in that scene and everything you can see, hear, taste, smell and feel. Whilst taking it in, can you squeeze your finger and thumb together three times and repeat three times. Brilliant. Keeping your eyes closed, can you tell me what positive impact the journey to this future point in your life has had on you?"

"I'm healthier, mentally and physically. I have a glow about me. I am more open to things than before. I am calm and at ease with life. I am secure in myself and my relationships with others."

"What positive impact did it have on your colleagues, friends and family?"

"We are closer. There are no barriers or pretences, people are more open with me, and more challenging, but not in an aggressive way. They seem more curious, more inter-ested in my opinions. There's more deep and meaningful two-way conversation with people. My relationships with people seem a lot easier and at the same time a lot richer. It's what I've always wanted but haven't always felt I had."

"What positive impact has the journey had on your career?"

"I have a global role with a global brand. I am still travelling but not as much and it is business class travel to different countries for a week at a time rather than driving or getting the train all over the UK almost every other day. Overall, I don't travel as much, and when I'm not travelling I mainly work from home. It's a bigger leadership role. It's more about increasing our brand value.

I'm leading the development of our culture, inspiring future leaders, being a brand ambassador for a healthier way to lead an organisation and a healthier way to live. I still work in the health industry and in the future I role model positive health-based values."

"What are you skilled at that you were not back in 2019?"

"Honestly, Claire, I am more skilled at everything. I have applied the knowledge and skills I had more effectively. The critical thing is that I have learnt to manage my emotional responses more effectively. I am also more skilled at managing my needs alongside the needs of others. I have boundaries. Oh, and I have become much better at living in the present, not ruminating over the past or worrying about the future."

"I hear what you say about not ruminating about the past. For the purposes of learning, can you imagine this future you turning to look back at you as you are today? What were the important changes you had to make in order to get to this point in the future?"

"Do you know, Claire, the main thing that jumps out at me is that I had to ask for help; I had to be vulnerable. I had to let go of some of the parts of me that have got in the way and stopped me achieving more and being happier."

"That's interesting, Laura. What parts did you have to let go of?"

"I have had to let go of 'The Fighter' in me. Not the resilient part that works well for me but the fighter who seems to be constantly ready for battle and assumes there is going to be one around every corner. This part of me is exhausting."

"I can imagine it is. You said parts... what other parts do you want to let go of?"

"The fiercely independent part of me. Again, it's not the part of me who is capable of being on my own and managing things when I need to. I mean the part of me that won't let others in, not fully in. The part that doesn't want to appear vulnerable, weak or needy. The part that wants to demonstrate I know what I'm doing. This part makes me feel frustrated with myself and yet I know I hold on tight to it."

"Are there any other parts, Laura?"

"Yes, the part of me that feels I have to make sure everyone around me is okay. I feel responsible for people even when I'm not. I feel like I can't relax until everyone is okay and everything is done. Does that make sense?"

"Yes, it makes sense to me, Laura. Is there anything else you needed to let go of?"

"Yes, I'm not sure if this is a part of me or almost an imposter who has taken over me lately, since the breakdown of my marriage to 'Fuckwit'. I used to be optimistic and trusting of people and now I feel cynical towards people and I feel a loss of my natural optimism. I think I feel so let down by him and by me for trusting him. When I look back, I knew he was a fake but didn't want to accept it. Now I don't trust myself with people and that makes me feel a little hopeless, I guess. It's also affecting my confidence at work."

"We can work on this too, Laura. When you look back, what do you think could have derailed you, but thankfully didn't?"

"I think it's the last bit: being cynical, losing hope, not trusting people. I feel I need people to help me. I need you to help me. I need to trust you. I know I can't change without help and support and I'm sure that will need to be from more than just you and I'm a little scared that I have put up some fairly big walls lately. I've never let many people in before as it is, and now I feel the walls are higher and thicker than before."

"You have already done well, Laura; you are letting me in, and I will not let you down. Now I want you to imagine walking back to the present and turning around to face the future. What actions do you need to take, that you are not taking now, to make this vision of your future a reality?"

This question makes me pause. "Honestly, I don't know exactly what I need to do. I hadn't thought about it before today, but the biggest thing, I guess, is to let go of those parts of me that I spoke about and to trust you and this process. I also need to look after myself better physically and mentally.

"In terms of specific actions, I want to go home and clear the house of anything connected with 'Fuckwit'. I want to make my home my home again and fill it with new life. I want to buy some plants and change the candles for some new scents; change some of the rooms around a bit. I have wanted to decorate my bedrooms and bathrooms ever since moving in. I think I would like to get the decorator in to help me give the place a refresh. Maybe if things around me are refreshed I might feel more refreshed. Do you know, I feel better just thinking about it."

"That sounds great, Laura. I can hear in your voice and see in your face and body a sense of optimism already. You seem so much brighter than when we started. Other than help from me, what help will you need and from who?"

"I will need the support of my daughter, Abi. She has been amazing over these past couple of months. She is there for me, no matter what mood I am in. She brings me up when I am down and when I need a pity party for a while, she parties with me, for just long enough for me to get the hurt out and move on for a while longer. Although... I don't want to be a burden to her. I want to be her mum; I don't want her to think she has to look after me. I need to change the dynamic of my relationship with a couple of my friends and be prepared to ask them for help too."

Superpowers & Highest Potential Self

After the Visioning exercise Claire describes the core characteristics of what she calls our Highest Potential Self (HPS). She says she likes to think of the HPS as the superhero inside all of us.

She says, "Our Highest Potential Self is when we have such balance in ourselves that that we are: Calm, Clear, Confident, Curious, Courageous, Creative, Compassionate, Connected and believe we have Choice over our circumstances. You may notice I like a C – word. Calm is my favourite C word. Calm is the foundation, as I notice that once we find our calm we are more able to access the others.

If you watch the Wonder Woman film, you will see that Wonder Woman embodies these characteristics. I like to think about these C - words as nine superpowers.

Claire talks me through a summary of the superpowers, what they mean, a quick technique for accessing some of the state that is the superpower, a symbol for easy recall and a quote.

Pages 50-67 describe the summary she gave me.

SUPERPOWER - CALM

Meanings

Without strong emotions – Neutral State.

Neither one end of the spectrum of emotions or the other.

Quick Technique

Breathe, inhale for 4, hold for 4, exhale for 4 – and repeat. Focus on breathing until calm.

Count backwards or think of countries with your initials in.

"Your calm mind is the ultimate weapon against your challenges"

BRYANT MCGILL

"Peace comes from within. Do not seek it without"

BUDDHA

SUPERPOWER - COMPASSION

Meaning

An ability to sense suffering (of self or another), reflect on how to reduce that suffering and enact behaviours to reduce the suffering.

Quick Techniques

Compassionate people put the needs of others as a priority and act to reduce the suffering of others.

If you need is paramount turn the compassion towards yourself, reflect on how to reduce your suffering and take action to reduce it.

"Compassion and tolerance are not a sign of weakness, but a sign of strength."

DALAI LAMA

"When we give ourselves compassion, we are opening our hearts in a way that can transform our lives."

KRISTN NEFF

"Teach this triple truth to all: A generous heart, kind speech and a life of service and compassion are things which renew humanity."

BUDDHA

SUPERPOWER - CURIOSITY

Meaning

A genuine desire to understand. Seeks to understand rather than make assumptions and judgements. Openminded and wanting to learn.

Quick Techniques

Curious people ask lots of questions of themselves and others. They also listen to learn from the answers.

Just for laughs, funny scene demonstrating curiosity

https://youtu.be/5x0PzUoJS-U

"We keep moving forward, opening new doors, and doing new things, because we're curious and curiosity keeps leading us down new paths."

WALT DISNEY

"A dog is not considered a good dog because he is a good barker. A man is not considered a good man because he is a good talker."

BUDDHA

SUPERPOWER - CLARITY

Meaning

The ability to think clearly and make the invisible visible.

Quick Technique

Practise 'The Wheel of Awareness' mindfulness exercise to open up your awareness.

https://www.wheelofawareness.com/

"Clarity is the moment we see without opening our eyes."

STEPHANIE BANKS

"To keep the body in good health is a duty... otherwise we shall not be able to keep our mind strong and clear."

BUDDHA

SUPERPOWER - CREATIVITY

Meaning

The ability to transcend traditional ideas, rules, patterns, relationships, or the like, and to create meaningful new ideas, forms, methods, interpretations, etc.

Quick Techniques

Be playful, silly and random.

Laugh out loud, add colour and metaphor and let go of things.

Let go of things.

———

"Creativity is intelligence having fun."

ALBERT EINSTEIN

———

SUPERPOWER - COURAGE

Meaning

To be brave enough to do what you believe in even if it frightens you.

Quick Techniques

Understand what frightens you to reduce the fear.

Reframe fear as opportunity.

"Courage is resistance to fear, mastery of fear, not absence of fear."

MARK TWAIN

"You only lose what you cling to."

BUDDHA

SUPERPOWER - CONFIDENCE

Meaning

Belief in one's own abilities.

Quick Techniques

Do the "Success Tapes" exercise.

Ask for feedback.

Play to your strengths.

Outsource what you were never meant to be good at.

"Confidence is that feeling by which the mind embarks in great and honourable courses with a sure hope of trust in itself"

CICERO

"Believe nothing, no matter where you read it, or who said it, no matter if I have said it, unless it agrees with your own reason and your own common sense."

BUDDHA

SUPERPOWER - CONNECTION

Meaning

An ability to connect to what is known, what is real, what is here and now and what really matters to you.

Quick Techniques

Disconnect from your technology and connect with what is going on inside you and around you.

Do the 'Grounding' Exercise (page 36).

"The TV won't work if the cable is not connected"

ANON

"If you are quiet enough, you will hear the flow of the universe, you will feel its rhythm. Go with this flow. Happiness lies ahead. Meditation is key."

BUDDHA

"I define connection as the energy that exists between people when they feel seen, heard and valued; when they can give and receive without judgement; and when they derive sustenance and strength from the relationship."

BRENE BROWN

SUPERPOWER - CHOICE

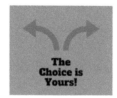

Meaning

An act of choosing from a range of options.

It's what makes us human. The superpower of choice!

Quick Technique

We always have a choice and sometimes several options.

If nothing else, you have choice in how you choose to respond physically, emotionally and mentally to any given situation.

Use this gift often.

"The content of your character is your choice. Day by day what you choose, what you think and what you do is who you become."

HERACLITUS

"Attitude is a choice. Happiness is a choice. Kindness is a choice. Giving is a choice. Respect is a choice. Whatever choice you make, makes you. Choose wisely."

ROY T. BENNETT

Claire tells me that she will help me to develop my super-powers, my HPS and my superhero self. She promises to help me to become calmer and more at ease, which in turn will help me to achieve more for less. It sounds too good to be true and yet she has me hooked.

She passes me a couple of laminated cards. The cards depict the HPS as being when you are neither in Survival mode or Reward and Acquisition mode.

Claire explains neither of these modes or states are healthy for us if we stay in them for too long. When in these modes our body and brain is dysregulated.

Being in a mode of HPS is healthy. Our body and brain is regulated. When in this mode we tend to make better decisions and achieve better outcomes.

Highest Potential Self[1]

Figure 1.

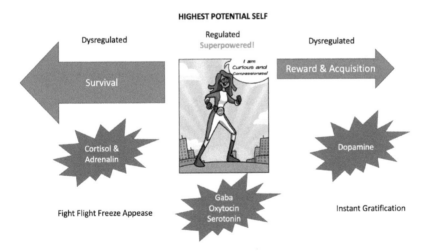

Figure 2.

Claire points out cortisol and adrenalin are released when in survival mode, in order to make us physically able to defend ourselves from the threat of a perceived attack. These neurotransmitters are fine in small doses, but too much is unhealthy for us. She describes the release of dopamine when we achieve gratification. Apparently, dopamine is addictive, which is why we are drawn into a constant craving for more of whatever gave us the dopamine release. Dopamine is another neurotransmitter which is best in small doses. This makes so much sense. When I'm not feeling like I have to defend myself, I am looking for ways to make me feel regulated and the more instant the better. My 'go to' reward cravings are sugary foods, alcohol, physical pleasure and buying things I don't need.

Claire is going to help me find my superpowers and instead of releasing so much cortisol and adrenalin I will apparently release more gaba, oxytocin and serotonin. These are neurotransmitters which are healthy 'Happy Hormones'. It's all good stuff to know and I want to get started on the practical application of what I am learning.

My Homework

Claire invites me to take an assessment of my self-compassion and encourages me to start a regular mindfulness practice to increase my self-compassion should I want to. She explains that increasing my self-compassion will help me to be more compassionate towards the different parts of me that show up as well as towards other people. She says she will email me some links. I'm starting to realise there is a lot to do outside the coaching sessions if I want to make real change, which I do!

Claire also suggests I reflect in a structured way every day and gives me a simple six-minute exercise for this. I will include this as part of my journaling.

Daily Reflection Activity[2]

3 minutes

Write whatever comes to mind when reflecting on the day.

2 minutes

Read what you wrote and write what insights you get from this.

1 minute

Read what insights you wrote and decide if you want to take action as a result. Write down what actions you want to take.

Link to Dr Kristin Neff's Self-Compassion assessment https://self-compassion.org/test-how-self-compassionate-you-are/.[3]

Links to Self-Compassion Guided Meditations – https://self-compassion.org/category/exercises/#guided-meditations.[4]

I'm leaving the coaching session feeling a sense of relief, as though my load has lightened. It was therapeutic and yet not at all like the therapy or counselling I have previously endured. I feel better already, a little faith in humanity has been restored, as well as faith in myself and my future. I am pleased with my choice of coach and for allowing myself to open up to Claire, although I think Claire made that easy. I am looking forward to practising my new super-powers and becoming more like Wonder Woman.

1. The grounding exercise on senses.
2. Vision of Your Ideal Future

Journal, Day 77

L ast night's 'Daily Reflection Activity'

3 minutes

Write whatever comes to mind when reflecting on the day.

My meetings were great, and we made good progress. I reminded myself to be grateful for working with people I like and respect and for doing work that I feel makes a difference.

I loved walking through London and catching taxis and the Tube, being here, there and everywhere for a full and productive day. I noticed how many people looked tired and miserable and yet again it was a reminder to me of how blessed I am that this is no longer my daily routine. It's great for one day but the thought of getting on this train every day to get into London five days a week and then doing the commute home is appalling. I look back and wonder how I used to do it almost every day, years ago.

I was a single mum. Abi was ten. I dropped her off for the school bus at 7.00am to get the 7.20 train to arrive at my office at 9am or later. After a stressful day at work, I would pick her up from the childminder at 7.30pm or later and heat myself some tea in the microwave whilst catching up with Abi, her day, her homework and bath and bed. No wonder people look tired and miserable; I think I was tired too back then.

I had a late lunch with the amazingly glamorous and lovely Cheryl. We had a good old girly chat and a tasty and healthy lunch, although I had a glass of wine with it. That's drinking during the day, twice in two days. I know at some point I need to stop and get my shit together in terms of healthy eating and not drinking but it's not like I am going totally off the rails. It is just that I have been so anal about calories and health etc. for the last few years that it feels naughty. My 10st 7lbs target is nowhere near a reality.

Andrew was supposed to call Thursday to rearrange meeting up with me. I can't imagine myself being a millionaire's girlfriend anyway. I do not want to chance being let down again. He was never there for me last time, not when it mattered, and he probably wouldn't be if we started things up again. He may have millions, be *incredibly interesting and all that, but I'm letting him go. I should never have texted him last month. It was a moment of weakness after a few wines at my last 'pity party'.*

2 minutes

Read what you wrote and write what insights you get from this.

1. *I still love my work.*
2. *I have better 'work / life balance' than I used to have and I am grateful, but I am still tired and a little miserable. I try to make myself better with alcohol and food and it's making me worse not better. I am frustrated that I am doing this and am unhappy with the results. I need to find something healthier to make me feel good about myself.*
3. *I can't believe I'm even allowing myself to think about dating again. Especially not an ex! I need to be happy with myself first.*
4. *I've been trying meditation and mindfulness (I think they are the same thing) and I'm feeling more grounded than I was a month ago. But I am still fundamentally a bit of a mess.*

1 minute

Read what insights you wrote and decide if you want to take action as a result. Write down what actions you want to take.

1. *Keep a focus on what I am grateful for as this helps me feel happier.*
2. *Stop daytime drinking!*
3. *Start eating more healthily!*
4. *Focus on me being happy and not me being happy because I find another man!*
5. *Continue with the mindfulness/meditation practice.*

I'm finding the reflection exercise each night brings up the same things over and over again. I am full of good intentions and some days I am really on it, but then it only takes something to come through the post about the Financial Settlement or someone at work to let me down and I am triggered all over again into a bitter, angry, hostile mess, thinking I am on my own and it's not fair and the world is against me. I sometimes remember to do one of the mindfulness exercises when this happens, and it helps in the short-term, but I feel there needs to be a more fundamental change in me. I try to think myself into the superpowers of the 'Highest Potential Self', but I tend to get frustrated with myself. I hope the coaching session with Claire tomorrow helps me learn some techniques to access these superpowers more effectively.

Doing the reflection exercise every night (well, almost), has helped me realise that my friendships tend to be quite shallow. I have started to open up and show more of my vulnerable side to Bridget and Louise and this has been really helpful. It feels as though they are opening up to me too as a result and our conversations run deeper than they did. I find myself sensing their support even when they are not with me. This is good. I feel a little less alone on a day-to-day basis. I have people who care enough to listen to me rant on and on and at least I have been less of a burden on Abi in this regard.

At the weekend I watched the Wonder Woman film, the one from 2017 that Claire recommended. It wasn't what I had expected, although I loved it, as she thought I might. This version of Wonder Woman is, as daft as this sounds, real. She is still stunning. She is far more beautiful than the version from the seventies (sorry, Lynda Carter). I want to be this version of Wonder Woman even more. She is a bit of a feminist. I loved the bit where she talks about men being unnecessary for female pleasure (I think all the customers of 'Ann Summers' toy department would agree). Men are unnecessary for most things when you are a capable woman. She isn't a man hater, though. She falls for Captain Steve Trevor. And who wouldn't, he's gorgeous. I know it's just a story of romance and it's not real, but it made me think a little more optimistically about love still being out there for me, somewhere. Having said all this, her bloke dies at the end, so that's not so great.

What I found compelling was her character. She's confident, courageous, curious and compassionate. She is also clear, and calm. What was the other 'C' superpower Claire talked about? That's it... creative. Well, she was certainly creative with that lasso she knocked everyone out with. The Lasso of Truth they called it. I wish I had had one of those when I was with 'Fuckwit': I never would have married him. The lasso forces anyone it captures into submission; it compels its captives to obey the wielder of the lasso and tell the truth. She also adopts the superpower of choice. She thinks and responds after weighing up her options. Even in the midst of battle she seems to do this. Claire was right. Wonder Woman basically has all the characteristics of the HPS. That's interesting. If they are good enough for Wonder Woman then they are good enough for me.

I also love Wonder Woman's sense of purpose. I've lost some of mine recently, since the split with 'Fuckwit'. My main purpose has been survival, and not going mad. I think I've been focused on survival for a long time, even before 'Fuckwit'. Probably as long as I can remember. I've survived some childhood trauma and some fairly traumatic events with husband number one and some crap at work in a couple of previous roles. It's not been easy being a woman.

I liked Wonder Woman's little phrases too, such as, "I will fight for those who cannot fight for themselves." And, "Now I know that only love can truly save the world. So, I stay, I fight, and I give, for the world I know can be."

I think I also saw the second quote on Claire's website. It's very inspiring. It's optimistic and I like that. I think after 'Fuckwit' I became quite cynical and pessimistic. I don't like being like this. I want to be more purpose driven and optimistic like Wonder Woman. I'm going to share my thoughts with Claire this afternoon. In the meantime, I had better engage my 'HPS' and get to the office.

Coaching Session Two

This time we meet at an office Claire has arranged for the session. When I arrive, Claire is sitting in one of two large, comfy armchairs with a lovely green tartan print. I have a feeling she works from here a lot as she seems very relaxed and at home. She stands up as I enter the room and gives me a big hug. I am caught a bit off guard as hugging isn't the norm for me, but I like it. It is as though we are old friends meeting up. Much like friends do, we start by complimenting each other. Me complimenting Claire on her lovely new blue jacket and Claire commenting on my new post marriage split hairstyle, saying how much the shorter do suits me. After a couple of minutes of general chat about life, we settle down into the session.

Claire asks me to share my reflections, insights and progress since the last session and she seems pleased with the openness I have towards everything. I share with Claire my low self-compassion score. It is 2.14 overall. Claire reassures me we will work on this throughout the sessions.

I am glad to get this off my chest. I have been anxious about sharing it. I feels a bit pathetic having such a low score. I am so used to being a high achiever in most things I do.

Claire suggests we start with another mindfulness type exercise. The purpose of the exercise is to help me to be present, centre myself and access the superpowers of my HPS. This is all about creating a more open and yet focused mind – a body that is calm and at ease – an open and compassionate heart.

Wholehearted Listening - An Exercise to centre your mind and body[1]

I invite you to sit up straight and position yourself comfortably in your chair. Feel your feet firmly planted on the ground and sense the chair supporting you. Check that your shoulders are relaxed, your hands are open, either on your lap or otherwise, facing up or down and definitely open.

You can close your eyes or lower your gaze and find a focal point to look at...

Access the part of you that listens with one ear where your focus and attention is on something else whilst at the same time trying to listen. I am speaking to you. You are hearing the words and getting most of what I am saying, though you really aren't taking it in at a very deep level and making sense of it.

Perhaps this part of you even looks like one small ear. As I'm talking to you, your mind is wandering... thinking about other things are more important to you. If your eyes were open you might even glance at your phone to see if you have any notifications or to check on the time. You may look out of the window to see what's going on. You might start wondering what others are doing.

I invite you to ask that one small ear part of you to move to one side. Thank it for its help and let it know that it comes in handy when you have many things in your mind and you don't need to focus very deeply on what someone else is saying.

Now I would like to invite you to go inside your heart and sit listening to me with the doors of your heart flung wide open. From this place you are able to listen with compassion and curiosity... you are calm and connected. As a result, you are able to listen deeply. There is nothing else that you can hear or think about except for my voice and the words that I'm saying to you right now. You are hearing what I say, the changes in tone, the energy and the intent behind what I'm saying. Your whole body is translating the emotions from behind the words and creating meaning from the message. You absorb my message through many senses. I invite you to continue listening in this whole-hearted focused way.

Whilst maintaining an open heart, bring focus to your breath... Follow it in and out...

Breathe a little deeper than the time before and exhale a little deeper... Bring your focus to your open heart and as you sit inside it, visualise the ember of a fire in front of you... Imagine your breath is stoking the ember... and with every breath in, the ember begins to grow stronger... brighter... warmer... And with every breath out, invite the warm bright calmness... compassion... curiosity of your heart ember to begin to radiate 360 degrees throughout your body and into the world.

Now invite all the different parts of you into your heart. Imagine they are sitting around the warmth of the ember with you... and invite them to bring focus to their breath... follow it in and out...

Breathe a little deeper than the time before and exhale a little deeper... bring focus to your open heart and as you sit beside each other visualise the ember of the fire in front of you... imagine your breath is stoking the ember... and with every breath in, the ember begins to grow stronger... brighter... warmer... And with every breath out, invite the warm bright calmness... compassion... curiosity of your heart ember to begin to radiate throughout your bodies and into the world.

And now, in your own way and at your own pace, I invite you to slowly open your eyes and return to the room.

Wow, I love that. I feel so open and safe. I feel like I want to open up to Claire and to myself. I feel like I am ready to engage with the parts of me that frustrate me. They frustrate me because they cause me problems, yet at the same time I struggle to let go of them because I also believe they have helped me achieve my successes at work.

Claire encourages me to stay centred as she walks me through a process to get to know these parts. I'm curious.

The Fighter Part

She starts by saying, "As I ask you questions, I want you to focus your attention inside you and notice any thoughts, feelings or sensations that show up. You may notice physical sensations. They may be pleasant or unpleasant. You may notice one feeling or many feelings. You may hear one thought or many thoughts competing with each other. You may notice blankness or fogginess inside. Whatever you notice, however strange or silly, this is all okay. Let me know what is going on for you and I will be able to make sure you are okay whatever comes up. Any questions, Laura?"

Claire looks at me closely and raises her brow a little in a way that suggests she is checking I understand what she is saying. I think I do, and I say so. I am comfortable asking Claire if I get stuck or confused.

Claire also says, "You may also notice your mind wanting to distract you and shift your focus away from a sensation, feeling or thought. Try to stay centred and rather than shift your focus, be curious about whatever you notice. What does it want you to know? What insight is it holding for you?"

I am curious, as this is so different from any previous coaching I have experienced. I tell Claire I want to work on letting go of the angry part of me, the part I've previously described as 'The Fighter'.

Claire nods. She says, "Laura, I invite you to tap into your superpowers and go inside you. Get a sense of what you described as 'The Fighter' part you said you want to let go of when we did the Imagineering the Future exercise."

"Yes, of course," I reply, eager to get on and sort out this part of me once and for all.

It takes me a while to notice anything happening. Then a memory comes to me. From this memory I can describe what it is like when it happens.

I say, "This part of me is always angry, and it's exhausting. I feel like it is almost always there, waiting in the wings. It is expecting to have to come out and defend me, stand up for me, make sure people don't knock me down. It feels like life is unfair and it wants to stand up for me." I sit back in my chair, relieved at having spoken this aloud.

"How much of your mental time and space goes to this part?" Claire asks, making a note of my response.

"It gets lots of it. Maybe twenty percent and then probably another twenty percent is on the part of me that is stood at the other side, in the wings. The one that is telling me I'm not good enough and I need to try harder. The one that picks fault with everything I do. The two of them together seem to have been such a big part of me for so long."

I can hear the exhaustion in my voice as I share this with Claire. I feel them like a heavy burden, weighing me down. Claire gives me a knowing look. I feel like she senses exactly how I am feeling, without having to say anything.

She talks confidently to me and in turn I feel reassured and confident in her.

"Laura, shall we get to know the angry part, 'The Fighter' first, and then the part that says you're not good enough? Notice where this angry part is located, on or around your body. Do you see it or perhaps feel it? Or do you sense it in some other way?"

I'm not sure I know how to respond. Rather than panic I take a few breaths to keep me grounded and then I feel something.

I pause for a moment and I focus on the sensations in my body. "Yes, I can feel it."

"Where exactly do you feel it, Laura?

"In my chest and my neck and throat."

"What do you notice about that?"

"When I think about it, this is exactly what it feels like when I get angry. It's like a fire breathing dragon and the fire is built up energy that has to come out. It's as though I can hear the dragon shouting its frustration at not being heard. When I'm angry, it's like the fire is actually coming out of me. I'm the fire breathing dragon! That's why my chest, neck and throat feel hot and sore."

Claire shifts forward in her chair with her pen poised ready to make another note. "Are you saying you can see the fire breathing dragon?"

"Yes, it's in front of me to the right."

"Laura, is this the same as 'The Fighter' part, you have previously described?"

"Yes, yes, She IS the fighter part. It's a really clear picture. Wow. I didn't expect that."

Claire smiles directly at me. I take it that I am doing this right, and she is happy with me.

"This is good, Laura. You said she is frustrated at not being heard. Would she like you to listen to her now?"

"I'm not sure. I think so. There is no fire at the moment. She is just sitting there patiently as though for the moment she is happy I have noticed her."

"How do you feel towards her, Laura?"

"I feel sorry for her. She looks exhausted. Probably from all the energy it takes to create fire."

"How old do you think the dragon is?"

Now I sit back bemused. How old is she? Then the answer just pops into my head. "She's almost as old as me."

"How old does she think you are? Can you ask her?"

LAURA'S PROTECTOR PARTS   89

I'm puzzled. Does Claire want me to ask out loud a question to this dragon in my mind's eye? I ask the dragon in my head instead. It works. As daft as this sounds, she answers back.

"How weird. She thinks I am about five years old. It's as though she is showing me a picture of me. I can see myself at five years old and surrounded by adults and being ignored."

"It isn't weird. You're really good at this. Is there anything you want to say to her?"

I think for a while. What would I like to say to her? I look at how exhausted she is, slumped down on her back legs, all wrinkly and old and sad.

"I feel like I want to tell her she doesn't need to generate the fire anymore. I feel like I want to say, you can retire, I've got this now."

"Okay then, let the dragon know that you're grown up now. Offer to show her around your life. Let her see that you have the maturity and confidence to be heard and understood."

Claire was right about sometimes feeling a bit silly and odd. This is the strangest experience and yet I'm going with it and thoughts and feelings keep coming to me.

"I'm showing her me standing speaking to people in suits in client meetings, chairing meetings, and she sees me at home with Abi. She's clapping for me, cheering me on. She's saying, 'go girl'. She's proud of me... I want to tell her that I don't need her to stand up for me and that I have the skills to speak up for myself."

"Okay, let her know this then." Claire takes a few large gulps from her water bottle whilst staying totally focused on me.

"I can feel some frustration building inside me. Whilst I'm grateful for her being there for me in the past, at the same time I'm a little annoyed with myself for not realising this earlier."

Claire looked up, head tilted to one side and made a quick note. "It's okay. That could be another part blending with you. You mentioned a part in the Imagineering your Future exercise. The part of you that is always telling you that you are not good enough could be a critical part trying to protect you from not being good enough. Does that resonate for you?"

It does resonate.

"It would have been difficult for you to have known this 'dragon' part of you in the same depth that you are getting to know it now, if you hadn't been through this process... Let's take a moment for you to take a few breaths and breathe in compassion for yourself and for this critical part. Be proud of yourself for having the courage to open up to these parts and to me. Thank your 'dragon' for being there for you when another, younger, less mature, less capable part of you needed her… Can you ask what your dragon fears?"

I sit quietly for a moment. "She's afraid that if she stops feeling angry, I will feel all alone again and without anyone to stand up for me."

"Is this likely, Laura? ARE you unable to stand up for yourself?"

"I'm more than capable of standing up for myself. I don't know why this part feels the need to take over me. If it stood back and gave me a chance to think, I would be able to find a way to resolve issues without needing her to take over. I just need her to give me that chance."

I can see Claire nodding ever so slightly. I'm encouraged to keep going.

"An example would be when someone at work doesn't appear to listen to me properly. This triggers me. I automatically feel disrespected and not valued. Instead of considering all the many scenarios that could be playing out, I jump straight to this one. Then when I get angry, I say the wrong thing in the wrong way and create bad feelings between us or I say nothing at all and allow my bad feelings about them to fester. This can often begin a ripple effect of unhelpful exchanges and a lot of wasted time and energy. I decide I don't need this person and start to isolate myself from them."

"What else does your angry part want you to know?" Claire asks.

"She wants me to know she was only trying to do her best for me, when no one else was listening. She says she is always there and will always listen to me."

"How do you feel about that?"

"That feels comforting. I like the idea that she is listening." I start laughing. "I have an image of her, The Dragon, sitting in a comfy armchair by a fire, reading... that's funny. I see her wearing reading glasses and she has an ear on what is going on with me and she's letting me know she can stop reading and help me out if ever I need her to speak up for me."

Claire also laughs with me. "What does she want for you, Laura?"

"She wants me to allow her to sit in the chair and be there for me, just in case I need her. She is afraid I will decide I don't need her anymore."

"Do you need her, Laura?"

"I definitely don't need her to take over me and breathe fire. That rarely helps me now. It's exhausting and often creates problems. If I need to get assertive or aggressive I am able to do that on my own. But I love the idea of having her there as a friend, someone who listens to me and stands by me to help me find my Highest Potential Self when I feel I am not being heard or understood. Now that would be amazing."

I find myself feeling like I'm having an out of body experience. Not a bad one – it's actually quite liberating.

"Is she happy to do this?" Claire says.

"Hang on, this is so odd. I'm feeling some flutters in my chest. I can feel my heart racing a little. She seems a bit upset. I think it's like I've criticised her for exhausting me and causing problems in the past. She really doesn't like it."

"Laura, what do you want to say to her?"

"I want to wrap my arms around her and tell her I appreciate she was only doing her best. I appreciate all she ever did for me because I'm doing okay. She has been a part of my history, my success to date and I'm thankful. I am also excited at the prospect of her still being around and with a different purpose."

"How is she reacting to this, Laura?"

"Ah, that's better. Yes, she like this, she is giving me a virtual hug back. She's okay; she's happy, in fact."

I am really getting into the process and ask Claire if we can explore another part of me. It's a part I didn't mention in the Imagineering the Future session but I know it is a big issue for me.

We take a break and when we come back to the session we start working on my Critical Part.

The Critical Part and the 'Know it all' Part

I begin, "I know I have a critical part. It's a part of me that is very tiring and makes me feel bad about myself. When I feel bad about myself I either drink, eat too much, over exercise or take it out on others."

Claire replies, "I understand. That's quite a normal reaction. We've all been there, Laura. Can you go inside again and see if you can find your critical part?"

"That's easy. She's always nearby. It's like I said before: I must have either the angry part or the critical part with me almost 50% of the time."

I can feel this part so easily and obviously now I am used to noticing sensations in my body. I can feel my heart beating faster. I can sense my body closing in on itself. I cross my legs high, thigh over thigh, and put my hands together in between my legs. I'm slightly bent over myself with head bent towards the floor. I close my eyes. Claire seems to notice me shift and accurately assesses that the part has taken over me.

"Would your critical part be willing to move in front of you so you can get to know it better?"

"Yes, it will. It wants to be seen as well as heard."

I have to sit up straight to look at it. This is not comfortable. I am a bit apprehensive. I think of Wonder Woman. I wonder how she would respond to this. I close my eyes again briefly and I emulate Wonder Woman's poise when she is reviewing her enemy. I take a few deep belly breaths. Wonder Woman would be calm, clear, confident, courageous, curious and compassionate.

"Looking directly at it, Laura, what do you notice?"

"I see a caricature of my mother. She is shaking her head at me in disappointment."

"Okay, how do you feel toward this part, Laura?"

"Okay. I know why she's there. She's trying to protect me. That's okay. She doesn't want me to be like her and fail, so she is making me work harder."

"It sounds like that's another part of you talking rather than your HPS. Can we try something?" Claire asks. "Would this part who seems to already know all about the critical part step to one side for now? We can listen to this part later. For now, we want to stay curious."

I think it is another part blending with me as I can feel myself tighten, I have a knot in my stomach, my breathing is in my throat and my palms feel sweaty. I give myself a little shake and find my 'HPS' posture. I take a couple of nice calming breaths and feel my breathing back in my belly. My hands are loosely on my legs again and my feet feel the floor beneath them. I think I am ready.

"Okay. Let me see if it will."

I am imagining this 'Know it all' part. It comes to mind as a teenage girl in a St Trinian's style uniform; you know, the rebellious schoolgirl who won't be told because she thinks she knows everything. She is scowling at me whilst moving slightly to my right but still in view.

"How do you feel towards the critical part now?"

"I feel compassionate and curious."

I notice Claire frowns a little as though not convinced. "Is she taking that in?" Claire asks.

"I'm not sure. I'm struggling to see the critical part. This 'know it all' part keeps taking over instead."

I can feel my shoulders are raised again and my arms are tingly. I can feel a pulsing vein at the right of my forehead. My jaw is clenched a little.

Claire offers, "I'm wondering if you have a part who is trying to help move things along?"

"What do you mean?" I reply.

"Is there a part of you that is trying to rush you through the process? Take a moment to ask inside."

How does Claire know what is in my head? She's done so many of these, I guess. She knows her stuff. I say, "Actually, there is. The knowing part wants to help you and me. She wants to speed things up and she wants to let you know she has learnt. She wants you to acknowledge her ability, to be impressed."

"Would you like to thank her? And ask if she would be willing take a break and watch us. We've got plenty of time and she may well learn more. I will be okay whatever comes up, even hard things."

"I'll ask... I think this part is around a lot. She wants to prove worthiness. She's been with me a long time."

"Okay, that makes sense." Claire says. "I bet this knowing part has been helpful to you at times. Our protective parts are there because they are trying to stop us feeling hurt in some way. They came in to protect us when we were younger, when we may have needed them more than we do today."

I summon my superpowers, I sit up straighter, move my bottom firmly to the back of the chair and relax my shoulders, feet flat on the ground. I remember what Wonder Woman says... 'Now I know that only love can truly save the world.'

"Laura, how do you feel toward this knowing part?"

"I love her. There have been times when my confidence has been low, and she has made me feel that I know what I'm doing and given me the courage to act."

"Okay, that's good. Let her know you are grateful for everything she has done for you."

I can see her smiling and blushing a little. "She likes that. She likes the recognition. She hasn't had recognition before."

"Is she willing to trust you? Is she willing to accept that you want to be curious and learn for yourself?"

I can see her shaking her head. I tell Claire, "She's not so sure about that."

"How old does she think you are?" Claire asks softly.

"About fourteen, I think."

"How do you feel about that?"

"It's interesting. She is the fourteen-year-old and wants to establish her place here, her value. This part is confused and thinks I'm her at age fourteen and she thinks you don't realise that I know what's going on with me. She thinks I've learnt the process from what we did with the last part so I can get on with it on my own. I feel like I want her to stop trying so hard."

"That makes sense. Laura, can you tell her you are a grown woman with a desire to be more open minded and to see that there might be more to learn and understand?"

I do this and give Claire a nod that I am ready to carry on.

Claire asks, "Would she let you help the fourteen-year-old you?"

I can see the rebellious teen in my mind's eye frowning and folding her arms tightly. I say, "She's confused by all this. She's always spoken up for me and feels strange about the idea of holding back."

Claire uncrosses her legs and lean forward slowly towards the screen.

"I hear she has taken the lead previously because she felt she had to. She wasn't aware of this superpowered Laura. She still believes you are a teen yourself who is not being recognised and valued for what she knows and what she can do. What's it like for this loyal and trusted part to meet the HPS you?"

"She's really surprised. She's feeling a bit concerned that she isn't valued now, much like the younger me she has been protecting."

"She doesn't have to go away. She will still be part of you. She's worked so hard for you she can stay and perhaps take on a slightly different role. Will she accept your help to do this?"

"She's thinking. She is tired. She wouldn't mind being able to retire on a beach somewhere with a phone so I can call it when I need reassurance that I know what I'm doing."

How do I keep coming up with these images? My imagination is normally quite useless.

Claire asks, "Are you happy to retire her in this way?"

"Yes, I am. I want to be able to find out more about my own capabilities, make some mistakes and feel the challenge of learning more for myself. I am open to the idea of being more vulnerable and asking for support when I need it rather than feeling like I have to rely on myself so much. After all, Wonder Woman has Steve and all the other Amazonian Women. If it's good enough for Wonder Woman, it's good enough for me."

"Fantastic. Imagine waving her off. She can enjoy a hard-earned rest."

I ask Claire if my 'HPS' is a state of mind or a functioning of my brain, and what the difference is. She tells me that 'HPS' is a state of mind and body, in which I can access the superpowers of calm, curiosity, confidence, courageousness, clarity, connectedness, compassion, creativity and choice. She tells me that to do this I need to take actions to integrate my brain so that I am regulated rather than dysregulated. If I am dysregulated I cannot access my 'HPS'.

"So, what is happening when my brain is dysregulated?" I ask, eager to know more.

Claire explains, "I am going to paraphrase something I picked up from Dan Siegal... *Where your body is regulated well or we might say, integrated, you communicate well, you have a balance in your emotions, you're flexible, you're insightful, you're empathic, compassionate, moral and have good access to intuition.*

"When a person is triggered into fight, flight, freeze, or even a disso-ciated state (for example, when they faint) the brain becomes prone to chaos and/or rigidity. The subcortical area of the brain is inter-acting with the cortical area in ways that aren't so helpful. When this happens, you can lose the qualities you had when you were regu-lated. You can lose all of them, or a few of them. And it can be really quick.

"Dan Siegal sometimes refers to this as *'the flipping your lid' state.* That's what we mean by emotion dysregulation. It's a non-integrated state of your brain.

"When this happens, your protective parts have taken over you or blended with you and in that moment their support makes you feel temporarily better but often with unhelpful consequences afterwards."

I can relate to this so much and I decide I want to learn more about this. I will ask Claire for more reading recom-mendations.

I say, "You mean like when I might stop listening to someone else's point of view because I am stressed and tired and just want to make a decision and get on with things. Then after shouting them down, I feel awful and have to apologise for how I spoke to them. And often I will reflect on my decision and realise I should have listened and slowed down my decision making."

"Yes, like that sort of thing," Claire says. "There might be several parts that want to be heard in this example. An impatient part, a part that feels misunderstood, or other parts."

I relax back into my chair. I shake my head a little. It's quite complicated but I am keen to learn more. I confess to Claire, "Yep, I am definitely dysregulated a lot of the time."

I wonder how I have achieved as much success as I have when I've been living this way for so much of my life. No wonder I am exhausted. I can feel my heart beating faster and my skin tingle at the back of my neck and in my hands. How much more could I be and how much more could I achieve if I learn how to regulate?

"Well, I definitely need this to work. So, how do I become regulated?" I ask.

"You're already on the path. This is why we do the grounding exercises and it's why I recommended you practise mindfulness. It's why I have been encouraging you to notice your body and move to a sitting or standing position

LAURA'S PROTECTOR PARTS   103

that enables you to feel your superpowers. All of these things help you to access a regulated an integrated brain and body, as the two are connected and mutually support regulation. Does this make sense?"

"Yes, I'm sorry," I say. "I know you have sort of told me this before. It's just a lot to process and remember. I've been going along with things because I trust you but now I really want to understand it. Not because I'm cynical – the opposite – it's because I'm really optimistic that this is going to have a huge impact for me."

"It is quite a lot to take in and yes, it is going to have a huge impact. I can tell that what we have been doing in terms of the grounding exercises and your practise with mindfulness and noticing any shifting in your body is all working."

I feel a smile of pride across my face, in response to Claire's comments and she smiles back.

"How can you tell it's working?" I ask.

"Well, for a start, Laura, you have been able to get your protective part that needs to demonstrate that it knows everything to step aside, despite it being a little afraid to do this initially. In stepping aside, it allowed your 'HPS' to be curious and ask for more clarity about what we are doing and how it works."

Claire continues, "Keep the questions coming. I'm happy to share as much as you want of the science behind what we do. That reminds me: I will send you a link to a TED Talk by Amy Cuddy and you can order her book directly from the link on my website. She has done research into body postures for generating different feelings and emotions to enable more positive outcomes. It's worth a read if you want to learn more and she's easy to follow."

My knowing part had been listening from a distance throughout and enjoyed knowing more. Claire started work again on my critical part.

She asks me, "Where do you notice the critic when it appears?"

I feel an irritation on my right shoulder, and I can sense my shoulders turn inwards and crunch upwards as if my whole body is trying to get rid of the irritation. It won't move and I have a sense of who this critic is. I imagine my mother, sitting on my right shoulder. I tell Claire, "It sits on my shoulder, like Jiminy Cricket in Pinocchio. I am seeing the cricket but feel like it's my mother."

"Could you ask him or her to sit down on the table so that you might address them face to face? How old do they think you are?"

I think for a while and a familiar image comes to mind.

"How weird," I say. "She thinks I am about seven. I can see myself at seven years old and I'm on my own in my bedroom, looking out of the window and feeling worthless, unloved and a bad person. I remember thinking that the girl who lived next door was so much more loved than I was, and it must be because she was pretty and well behaved and clever and polite. I saw myself as ugly, awkward, clumsy, not too bright and I know this is going to sound silly, but I have a distinct memory..." I break off.

Claire says encouragingly, "I promise it doesn't sound silly at all."

I find myself drawn into the memory...

"I feel so sorry for my seven-year-old self. She has convinced herself that one of the reasons she isn't loved is because she sometimes forgets to brush her teeth and the girl next door would never do this. My teeth are a bit yellow and the girl next door has lovely white teeth.

"I don't feel silly," I say. "I just feel sorry for my younger self and want to pick her up and tell her how lovely and lovable she is."

"That doesn't sound silly at all," Claire says. "Do you want to take the time to do this?"

I go inside myself and feel my seven-year-old self in my heart. My heart beats stronger and seems to fill my rib cage. I've rarely felt it this strong and whilst I sit patiently accepting this feeling, I notice it calm down and it's as though my heart gets smaller again and back to a normal size and heart rate. Claire watches me as I shift in my chair, blink a few times and stretch my eyes open and relax.

"Was there anything in particular that was going on around age seven that would have created this memory?"

"Yes, I know exactly what it was. It was the time my mum attempted an overdose. I knew about it, but no one ever spoke to me about it. I had been awake listening to all the commotion the night it happened. No one ever spoke about it in front of me and I didn't feel I could speak about it."

Claire looks directly at me. I feel like in that look she has reached over and hugged me through the screen. "I'm sorry to hear you had to experience that. If you want to we can explore this further another time, but for now are you okay to continue exploring the critical part?"

I am. I have been aware of this childhood experience for a long time and its likely influence on who I am and how I behave. I'm not afraid to unpack this with Claire at some point. I have had some counselling in the past hoping to work through this, but nothing ever worked. I think I didn't trust the counsellor's capability or intent. I think perhaps I just couldn't relate to them. With Claire it's different. I feel like she gets me. She's a success in her own right and she's 'worn the t-shirt' in term of her previous career in the corporate world and her life experiences. I have huge respect for this. She also referenced some of her own traumas in our Chemistry session. Her openness about her own life and work experience makes it easier for me to trust her, without her making it all about her.

I say, "Yes, I would very much like to explore my childhood experience with you and I'm happy to do this another time. I would like to continue exploring the critical part."

"Okay. If you become too uncomfortable as we work on this part, just say and I can help that part of you that feels uncomfortable. Can you let this critical part know that you're grown up now. Let her see you. Offer to show her around your life. See what she thinks."

Claire waits in silence as I go inside myself and sense the critical part. "She is a bit dismissive of my successes. It's as though she can't acknowledge them. I can hear her in my right ear saying, 'Ah, but you're still not with someone, you're still Miss Independent and having one-night stands and such rather than allowing yourself to heal and find someone you can commit to and allow to support you.' And she's right."

I can feel my entire body slouch under the weight of the criticism. Claire notices. I know she notices. I've started to appreciate her tiny facial gestures that demonstrate her empathy and compassion. I'm okay being emotionally laid bare like this. It feels safe.

Claire asks, "When you say she's right, is this your 'HPS' saying this or a part of you?"

That's a good question. I sit up and back into my chair again. I take a big deep breath. I roll my shoulders a few times and move my head from side to side releasing the tension in my neck. I twitch my nose and crumple my face. And with a big inhale and exhale I say, "It is my 'HPS' saying this."

"What exactly are you saying your critical part is right about?"

"There are other parts of me that are very much present in me. The part that has decided it is better to be independent rather than try to find love. The part of me that indulges in too much alcohol and one-night stands to numb against the loneliness of this decision. After all the recent heartache and previous heartache, it feels good sometimes just to disconnect from my emotions and the overthinking and just be in my body rather than my mind. Alcohol helps me do this and no strings sex is also a way to make my body feel good without having to think about anything else."

Wow, I feel better getting that out in the open. I haven't even admitted the one-night stand stuff to myself in my journal. I'm not judging myself and I don't feel judged by Claire either. God, this is refreshing!

LAURA'S PROTECTOR PARTS   109

Claire makes a quick note and then tells me we can come back to my thoughts on this after we have finished with my critical part, if this is something I want to do. And I do.

"Did your critical part see your 'HPS' being able to criticise your own behaviour?"

"Yes, actually she seems to be quite impressed for once."

"Great, whilst she's feeling this way, ask her if she is prepared to step aside for a while to allow you to work on these criticisms without her. Is she prepared to see what you can learn from working with me and hold back until we check in with her again at our next session?"

I can see the image of my mother considering this. She takes her time but eventually takes a seat, lights a cigarette and nods back at me, confirming she will do this. I know this part will need a lot more work, but I feel relief for this current reprieve from her and I tell Claire this.

"So, Laura, can you see how you have identified a number of parts of you that sometimes take over you or blend with you to some degree and limit your superpowers?"

I can. The process we have just been through make so much sense to me. It fills me with optimism. Already I feel more resourceful. I feel like with more help I can learn to get to know the various parts of me that I have allowed to limit my success and cause me unnecessary stress.

Claire asks if I would like to explore my earlier thoughts about some recent behaviour. I welcome the opportunity to share my thoughts. Claire never appears to judge. I feel safe to open up about behaviours that I might feel ashamed of sharing with others for fear of judgement.

"I've been drinking way too much lately, and this leads to me eating the wrong things and to hangovers which all impact my weight and my exercise regime and then make me feel altogether less than fabulous. Given I want to be feeling fabulous about myself by the time I am fifty, I need to stop this and lose this extra weight I am carrying and get fitter."

Claire is quiet for longer than usual. We sit together in the silence. It's comfortable for me to be silent with Claire. Then I think, 'I bet that's another bloody part of me talking.' And Claire asks, "What makes you think you need to lose weight and be fit to be fabulous?"

Her question stops me in my tracks. I can't think for a while. I just have scrambled thoughts like chaos in my head. I shake my head and try again to answer. I can't.

"Laura, how about you shake more than just your head. You know I said we might do some stuff that feels silly; well, are you up for feeling silly but hopefully in a good way?"

I trust she knows what she's doing, and I let her know I am up for it.

"Laura, let's stand up. Let's shake our arms."

I can see Claire shaking her arms vigorously in front of her and then to the side and above her head. I'm curious so I follow her lead. Within seconds I'm laughing, not an embarrassed laugh but more of a relieved laugh. This is actually quite enjoyable.

"Now, let's see if we can shake our booties. What do they call this? Is it twerking?"

Claire is doing something that sort of resembles twerking but isn't and it is hilarious. She's not taking herself seriously and I feel compelled to laugh again and to have a go myself. I don't think I'm much better at it but again it feels great. We continue to do this whilst Claire talks me through the power of moving freely like this, without inhibition. I tell her perhaps I should try this instead of sex and we both laugh.

After a few minutes of shoulder shaking, sort of twerking, head banging and playing air guitar we sit down. I am feeling so energised and clear headed.

Claire repeats her earlier question. "So, what makes you think you need to lose weight and be fit to be fabulous?"

"It's the part of me that is trying to be loved and thinks that if I do these things I will be loved. It's a bit like my younger self believing that if I brushed my teeth more often, I might be loved. I know the reality is that I know I am not overweight. I could do with being a little fitter for the health benefits but not to be lovable. When I think about things whilst being my 'HPS' I can see things so much more clearly."

"Laura, what do you notice about how you are sitting?"

I scan my body in the chair. "I'm sitting with both my feet on the floor, my hands are gently on my thighs and slightly open and upward facing. My shoulders are back and down in a comfortable way, not tense or extended. I'm sat with my back against the back of the chair and my rib cage is up and open, allowing me to breathe from my belly. Yes, and I am breathing deeper, taking more oxygen in."

"You are embodying your 'HPS'. You are able to see things with this clarity, this fresh perspective when your physical and biological state is regulated. That regulation has been achieved by all that shaking about to get you out of dysregulation when you couldn't think clearly. Then when you sat down again you sat in an 'at ease' posture which further enabled regulation. Does this make sense to you?"

It does make sense. I love how simple and quick it is. As quickly as I can get myself dysregulated, I can also regulate myself again. I'm so excited to practise noticing my state and changing it. Claire tells me the movement between being dysregulated and regulated is an important stage but that I don't always have to make it a full-on shake, rattle and roll. Let's face it, it won't always be appropriate to do this. She says I could think of the movement as a bit like the spin the eighties Wonder Woman did to change from Diana to Wonder Woman. She laughs and tells me I don't need to change into a costume, but perhaps a bit of a shoulder roll, a face twitch or a stretch of my arms and legs will be enough. And if it isn't I can always suggest a loo break and go and have a full-on Wonder Woman Spin in a cubicle. I laugh to myself at the thought and promise to myself I will try this next time I find myself fully triggered. Claire also suggested I think up a mantra, a little saying I can say to myself to help access my superpowers and anchor the embodiment of my 'HPS'. I agreed to have a play with that over the next few weeks and see what works best for me.

We wrap up the session, booking another one a few weeks from now.

My homework

Another meditation/mindfulness practice. The wheel of awareness. https://www.wheelofawareness.com/.[2]

- Play around with a possible mantra to help access my superpowers and anchor my HPS.
- Daily Reflection Activity.
- Practise noticing how my body shifts and how this relates to shifts in my thinking and emotions and note this in my journal.
- Notice what parts show up and make a note in my journal.
- Focus my reflection exercise on:

1. What I notice in my body and how this relates to my emotions and thoughts.
2. Describing the parts that get triggered and what happens when they do.

LAURA'S
INNER
CHILD

Journal, Day 87

It's ten days since my second coaching session with Claire. I have been doing my homework.

The Wheel of Awareness

The Wheel of Awareness website is great. I have read the science behind the Wheel of Awareness meditation. I am starting to realise that meditation and mindfulness practices are pretty much the same thing.

The Wheel of Awareness is a tool to help create more well-being in your life. It helps you to focus and direct your awareness. The metaphor is that of a bicycle wheel, and all along the rim are four places where you can direct your focus, accessing those moments through a "spoke of attention." By practising moving between the hub (of awareness) via the spoke to specific senses, you can gain more control of your outcome.

There are four categories of senses:

- The five main senses: taste, touch, sight, hearing, and smell
- A sixth sense. We could call these body sensations: in the gut, our breath, heartbeat, muscles, bones, blood and so on.
- A seventh sense: mental activities such as thoughts, feelings, memories, beliefs, emotions, images, plans, and anything else we have on our minds.
- An eighth sense: interconnectedness; the ability to connect to yourself, those close to us, all other humans, and planet Earth as a whole, bringing compassion and kindness to others and to yourself.

I've been doing the Wheel of Awareness practice every day. It makes me feel like I am able to be less reactive to situations and I generally feel less distracted and overwhelmed. A good example would be the meeting with my boss yesterday. Sarah is someone who, despite being a brilliant MD, obviously struggles sometimes with her own insecurities. She always wants me to explain in detail why I am doing what I am doing. She also seems to have to find something to critique.

In our meeting, I felt I had presented her with a perfectly pitched business case for the new TV campaign with just the right level of detail for her (more than I would normally give anyone else). I had shared the presentation with lots of other stakeholders to make sure I had their buy-in and also to make sure I hadn't missed anything relevant before pitching to Sarah.

Despite all my preparation, Sarah still wanted more data to support the benefits case, a more detailed breakdown of the spend for the campaign and exactly what would be included in it. Normally I would feel myself react to this both physically and emotionally and this would give Sarah cause to focus on my reaction rather than her own behaviour. This time I was able to catch myself being triggered. As soon as I noticed my heart starting to race and frustration building in a tingling sensation in my arms and my body moving forward, I took a deep breath, let it out slowly and quietly. I rolled my shoulders and sat back in my chair, all very subtly, whilst slowing down my thought process.

Instead of thinking about my defence I got curious and asked Sarah a few questions to understand her needs better. The brilliant thing was that in thinking about my questions she eventually decided that actually she had everything she needed and thinking it through a little more had helped reassure her. I dodged a mountain of extra work there just by applying such a small change. I'm sure all the meditation practice has made this so much easier to do.

This week I received an email from my solicitor that outlined 'Fuckwit's' finance submission as part of the Financial Separation Agreement. On this occasion I didn't notice my bodily reactions, although they were kicking off all over. I was so focused on the lies he was clearly still telling, which made me think about all his lies in the last three years we were together. I went into a doom loop of anger which led to a couple of hours of not being able to focus on anything, eating a full tub of Ben and Jerry ice cream and drinking a bottle of wine.

If only I had noticed the start of the doom loop as my heart rate went through the roof and every muscle in my body pulsed with adrenalin and cortisol. I was like Mike Tyson preparing for the fight of his life. I wish instead of opening the bottle of wine I had remembered the Wonder Woman spin, popped on some eighties music and danced out those feelings then reconnected with my HPS with a quick session with the wheel.

I'm not downhearted though. I know I'm not going to get it right first time every time. I love this quote I heard from Dan Siegel, the originator of the Wheel of Awareness:

"Where attention goes, neural firing flows, and neural connection grows."

More practise and I will get better at this. My brain will rewire itself so that my automatic response when triggered will be to start a pattern of:

Notice, Movement, Mood, New posture, Mantra = Highest Potential Self.

NOTICE the sensations in my body

MOVE to rid my body of these sensations

Decide on a new MOOD, Emotion and Feeling I want and remember when I have felt this before

Position my body in the NEW POSTURE simulating my chosen memory

Repeat a helpful MANTRA

I've also identified a mantra for when I want to anchor myself in my HPS.

"I am Super Neuro Me!"

It's my shorthand for reminding myself that I have all of my superpowers at my request. I just need to relax into them. When I say this to myself it helps me to relax my body, and when I'm relaxed I can get connected, calm my thoughts and gain more clarity. I am more likely to be curious and ask questions, be more compassionate towards myself and others, be more creative in how I look at the situation and see the choices available to me. I am more likely to take action with confidence and courage.

Journal, Day 99

I have noticed my angry part, the fire breathing dragon, is finding it difficult to stay on that deckchair on her holidays. Sometimes she can take over me in entirety and once I have completed the pattern of - Notice, Movement, Mood, New posture, Mantra - I lovingly ask her to step away. Sometimes she shows up as a full-on fire breathing dragon and at other times she comes into my mind as an irritable dragon muttering under her hot breath. This is when she is less angry and more irritated or frustrated. Either way, I have learned to befriend her.

I have also noticed several appearances of the critical part. She seems to start talking to me every time I look in the mirror. I immediately start picking up on the fine lines around my eyes and the new ones above my top lip. Then it's like I want to punish myself further by checking my side view to see if my belly is sticking out and then a quick glance at my rear view to see how much my bum is sagging. The other day I went on to notice the stretch marks on my boobs and across the tops of my thighs. I have also noticed the negative shift in my mood when I do this and a pattern of self-sabotage as I reach for something sugary and sweet to make myself feel better.

Yesterday, I had a conversation with my critical part and asked it to chill out. I even said, 'Chill out mum,' and I reappraised myself through a loving, compassionate lens. I saw an hourglass figure, clear skin, decent sized boobs, some muscle tone in my calves and quads and in my arms. I felt so chuffed with myself that I went for an evening class at the gym! I don't normally go to the gym during the evening when all the properly fit people go. I normally pop out during the day when I work from home, which is when the mums tend to go. It's far less intimidating. Today my HPS showed up and I wasn't intimidated, I was confident.

I have noticed a new part. It's a part of me that is a bit too driven. When I get a bit stressed, a bit conscious that I have a lot on my plate, it's as though I'm in the centre of a tornado which sweeps up every other possible task I could ever need to do, and they all circulate around me so fast I can't concentrate on any of them to get them done. I don't know what's going on here. I want to ask Claire about it next time I see her.

Having said this, I generally feel a lot more in control of my emotions. This is a good thing because this weekend 'Fuck-wit' is coming to collect the last of his belongings from the house and I need to stay calm when I see him.

Journal, Day 104

I've just been on the phone to Cheryl organising our girls' weekend. We're off to Leeds for a weekend with some mutual friends from London, and Abi. I need more fun in my life. I've been putting in some long hours at work and quite a bit of travelling, at the same time as working on my self-improvement. Claire talked to me about living life more 'at ease' so I'm going to give myself a weekend off becoming a better version of me and have lots of alcohol, some naughty food and lots of laughs with the girls.

As I write this, I am aware that there is an implied criticism in my mind. I notice it and reframe what I just said to myself. I am going to become a better version of me by having fun, accompanied by some alcohol and some treat food. After all, I deserve it!

Journal, Day 106

Every day is just flying by and I haven't had time or made the time to write about the day. I am wondering if, in a way, this is a good thing, as I think I'm just getting on with life and not dwelling on the past or planning too much of the future. I am living in the present and I must admit I am enjoying it. I feel far less stressed. In fact, now I come to think about it I haven't felt stressed for a while. I was busy working last week. A couple of days in Dublin and various meetings in London and a full day in the office and a work's evening out in Leeds. By the time I'd worked, travelled and slept, there wasn't much free time for exercise or mindfulness practice and I haven't been eating well.

I need to find the right level of busy to stop me ruminating yet to also allow me time to plan healthy eating and exercise. I think I use being busy as a distraction from feeling sorry for myself. I need to talk to Claire about this. Maybe it's another part of me. I aim to have several good days this week with lots of exercise and a fresh green smoothie for breakfast every day, limiting my carbs and drinking lots of water.

Journal, Day 110

The finale to another hectic week was my weekend in Newcastle with Abi and some friends. It was so much fun, really laid back and spontaneous and I loved it. I didn't think about calories or money or anything other than once again living in the moment. Abi and I drove up to Newcastle on Saturday morning and met the others for lunch. They had caught the train up from London late on Friday night. We had a lovely lunch and chat over a couple of bottles of wine at a trendy bar by the quayside and then went back to our hotel.

At the hotel, we had cocktails and more wine before going to our rooms for a break and to change for our night out. I was already feeling tipsy and no wonder. I wouldn't normally drink this much over an entire day and evening.

I had bought a lovely sequinned white dress the day before, in between meetings in Leeds. It was quite expensive but looked so cute and girly and 'party, party' and I just thought, "What the hell?" I know I should stop spending so much but I just think, "Why not have what I want? I deserve it. I only have myself to answer to and I'm not harming anyone." The dress was so worth it, as I felt great and loads of people commented. Although I did feel a bit like the fairy on the top of the Christmas tree. I have promised myself I will be more spontaneous and less serious, and the dress made me feel fun and flirty and fabulous!

We had drinks in The Botanist, where Katie's cardigan was stolen. Fancy wearing a cardi for a night out, anyway! In between several more bars, we went to Jamie's Italian and shared two pizzas between the five of us for a bit of carb to soak up the alcohol. I needed it.

We ended the night in another bar, which was heaving. We couldn't really dance properly for bumping into people. I can't dance well at the best of times, but the number of people there made it impossible to throw any shapes. We had some photos taken in a booth like the ones in the supermarket but pimped up for a night club feature and charging twice the price, and then we left.

Back at the hotel, I poured a pint of water for me and Abi and we went straight to bed, after taking off our makeup and moisturising. I never forget to do this no matter how drunk I am. Cheryl admitted the next day that she slept in her contact lenses and make up and could not be bothered cleaning it off and putting it back on the next morning, so she had left it on. I could never do that. I feel I must wash my hair every day and cleanse tone and moisturise every morning and night. Having said that, the 'couldn't care attitude' Cheryl has is something to admire. I wonder if this is a perfectionistic part that I might need to work on. I will talk to Claire about it. I'm starting to notice parts cropping up all over the place. It's good though, because if I can learn to understand these parts better I can be better, happier, healthier and achieve more.

I didn't want the weekend to end. It was sad leaving the girls. They all live in and around London. I love Cheryl's fun spirit. I could learn a thing or two from her about living in the moment and being more relaxed about life. I want more of these girlie weekends and girlie nights out. I need the encouragement of others to let myself go, be silly and have fun.

Journal, Day 114 - Coaching session with Claire

We are online again today. I am feeling good. I tell Claire I have continued to practise the Wheel of Awareness meditations and I'm fairly consistently reflecting for at least the six-minute exercise every night in my Journal. I also say I have been using my new mantra "I am Super Neuro Me" to help access my superpowers and anchor my HPS. Claire explains part of 'the feel-good factor' will be the dopamine hits I am receiving as a result of doing what I commit to doing in terms of the practise. This is good. Dopamine is addictive, she explains, and therefore the more I practise, the more I will want to practise, and the more I practise, the more I will wire my brain differently to go from creating temporary positive states to permanent traits. Listening to this, I can feel my enthusiasm to keep going with the practise increase.

We start the main part of the session with what Claire describes as a priming exercise. This is good as although I am generally in a better place, I'm feeling a bit nervous about asking Claire about some of the other parts of me I have recently identified.

Priming Exercise

Take a piece of paper and brainstorm all of your positives...[1]

Start with the things you like about your age, gender and looks.

Go on to list the positives in terms of your education and life experience.

Write down your skills and work experience.

Make a note of your positive relationships.

Any other positives that come to mind.

Now read the list back to yourself... slowly... take in every positive... take it in through your eyes as you read the words on the page and through your ears as you hear your voice speak the words aloud. Notice how you feel as you go through the list. Anchor these feelings with a mantra such as "I am awesome" or "I am resourceful" or "I am me" or something of your own choosing.

We start by going back to some of the parts from last time, the angry part of me, in the form of the dragon that gets a bit shouty and aggressive. The know it all, impatient part of me that wants people to speed things up and looks a bit like a St Trinian's schoolgirl. And the critical part of me that comes to me as my mum, sitting on my shoulder, making me feel self-critical.

Claire helps me to know these parts better, understand how they are trying to help me, appreciate them instead of blaming them, and show them how I am capable of managing without them needing to take over me. I can see how in time they will witness how I am developing my superpowers. The more I learn to embody these superpowers, the less they will feel the need to take over me. Claire asks me to score myself against the superpowers over the past few weeks.[2]

Superpowers	Score 1-Never, 2-Rare, 3-Sometimes, 4-Often, 5-Almost Always	Comments
Curiosity	3	I've always been pretty good at this, although I have found myself judging people initially and having to remind myself to be curious.
Compassion	3	I've been trying hard with this. Curiosity definitely helps me to be more compassionate.
Calm	2	This is one of the hardest when I'm tired, under pressure of time, frustrated with people, angry, hungry, hungover, uncomfortable. I think calm is the first thing to be affected by all of these things and this triggers the others eventually.
Clarity	2	When I am not calm I lose clarity very quickly, I get overly focused and don't see the woods for the trees or I can't see anything for the chaos in my mind.
Creativity	2	I've always struggled with creativity. I think in fairly straight lines. I think it relates to my need for calm again. I think it also has something to do with not being prepared to let go of some parts of me that like to be in control and responsible and serious. Also, maybe when there is too much of my 'All knowing' part in me.

HPS Progress Review

Superpowers	Score 1-Never, 2-Rare, 3-Sometimes, 4-Often, 5-Almost Always	Comments
Courage	3	I have felt this fairly regularly but it's almost like it's on the surface rather than from somewhere deep inside me. I need to work on my preparedness to be vulnerable and out of my comfort zone.
Confidence	4	Despite everything and maybe sometimes because of everything I generally feel quite high in confidence. I believe in my ability to achieve.
Connection	2	My mind is normally in so many different places, I don't feel very connected. Mindfulness lately has helped me feel more connected and I know I need to do more work on this to help me stay calm, which then seems to link to increase everything else.
Choice	2	I am still not always making the wisest of choices because I am rushing all the time. I am not processing the fact that I have choice and applying that fact.

HPS Progress Review

Some of the qualities are beginning to feel quite natural, such as curiosity and confidence, although I've always been pretty confident. I think the difference lately is that I feel an inner confidence. Previously, I think, it's been more a part of me that has projected confidence in order to be heard and seen, the dragon perhaps on some level and maybe with a little of the all-knowing part. Lately it feels more like it is me and not my parts who is confident. I'm more confident because I am becoming more in control than the parts controlling me. I know it's early days, but it definitely feels like a shift.

Claire listens to me explain the shift in me and reassures me that as I continue to practise mindfulness/meditation and apply the discipline of:

Notice –Movement – Mood - New Posture – Mantra

I will reduce my parts' sensitivity to being triggered into their protector mode. She suggests I complete the HPS Progress Review every few weeks to track how I am shifting from state to trait.

Claire says, "Laura, the more you prioritise self-care activities, the more readily you will notice when a part is wanting to blend with you and take over from your HPS. This will give you time to choose to respond effectively, move and re-engage your HPS."

This makes sense. I am still a little confused about the different parts. I ask Claire to help me understand more about the difference between my HPS and my parts. She says my HPS is perhaps most simply understood as:

"...The you who is centred, grounded and loving, the You, who is not a part. We all have self-energy. We were born with it. Life experiences, however, encourage parts of us to emerge and they sometimes take over from our self-energy. All parts are with us for a reason. They all have good intentions. Parts either carry burdens from the past, often our 'inner child' parts, and other protector parts take on protective roles to protect the parts that feel a burden or are wounded by the past."

I wish I'd understood this years ago. This is why it is so valuable for me to notice when I feel dysregulated. On these occasions it is often because a part has taken over. Sometimes I make it easy for a part to take over. I have noticed it is easier when I haven't prioritised self-care activities such as:

- Going for a walk and embracing nature rather than moaning about the cold, mud, rain, smell of cow muck, tired legs, sore feet!
- Exercising enough but not 'overdoing it!'
- Stretching my body out to release tension from exercise or so much sitting at my desk and in meetings.
- Enjoying a healthy lunch, at the table rather than at my desk or on the run.

- Taking screen free time – that's laptop, phone, iPad, TV, Games Console.
- Having a long hot bath (even better a hot tub).
- Sipping a glass of wine and tasting it mindfully rather than glugging at it in desperation for the numbing effect.
- A girly chat with Bridget, who makes me laugh until I almost pee my pants.
- An early night.
- A sleep in.
- Great sex! (although this is off the table until I find Mr Right.)

As we continue with the session, Claire helps me get to know, understand and appreciate my part that is like a tornado. She helps me realise this is another protector part that creates the tornado of activity to distract my inner child from being hurt. It comes to protect me when my inner child is triggered into feeling wounded in some way. We also get to know my perfectionist part. This part is also there to protect my inner child from feeling hurt.

We work with both of these parts in the same way as we have previously. The process follows this sort of pattern:

Parts Process

1. Find the part - Where is it located in or around my

body? (The Wheel of Awareness has really helped me notice more what sensations I am feeling in my body.)

2. Focus on it - Go inside. (This is hard to do at first but gets easier with practise – my meditation practice is helping me connect more to what is going on inside me and to be calm and clear of distraction as I go through the next few stages in the process.)

3. Flesh it out - Get to know more about it. (I am naturally curious at this stage and I find my creativity is showing up as I imagine my parts as characters with voices. I see and hear them in detail.)

4. Feel toward it - (I find myself feeling mainly compassion here and wanting to know more. I am growing in courage and confidence as I separate from the part.)

5. Befriend it - (I treat my part as a separate entity from me and I treat it as I would any other person that I would want to build a high trust relationship with. I am transparent with it, I show it my HPS, and it grows its trust in my HPS.)

6. Find out what it fears will happen if it doesn't do its job. (I get to know its fears and let it know my HPS is able to let it relax those fears.)

I am getting to understand that some parts are protectors who feel it is their job to prevent hurt to my younger parts. They try to prevent wounds from being triggered. They try to manage my day-to-day life. These are the parts that sometimes, 'Try hard', 'Try to be perfect', 'Take responsibility' and 'Need to be in control'. They serve me well to a point, but when they over function they exhaust me and can create problems for me and for others on the receiving end of this part of me.

There are also protective parts that are quite extreme in their response. They take over me very quickly. They want to stop the pain that is activated when a younger part of me has an unhealed wound reopened. For me, these parts are the ones that get me to drink much more in one go than is healthy and when it's not about the taste but all about getting drunk and feeling nothing. Thankfully, this doesn't happen often. If it's not getting drunk it's spending way too much money on things I do not need or indulging in some other unhealthy behaviour that is all about distracting me from the pain inside.

Then there are the wounded or burdened parts that Claire helps me to understand. These are often young, vulnerable parts. They carry wounds, burdens, hurt, and sometimes trauma. They come to me as memories, sensations, emotions and deeply held beliefs I hold on to. I can see as a result of the work with Claire that these parts often feel shame, they represent unmet needs, a lack of love and loneliness. They are stuck in the past and have implicit memory. Parts are not their wounds, though. These parts are creative, sensitive, loving and playful without their burdens.

Inner Child Parts

Claire encourages me to go inside and find a part of me that my protector parts feel the need to protect.

I say, "I have an explicit memory of my brother pinning me down on the floor and I am not able to breathe. This young me feels like not only is she being pinned down and under attack but also that no one cares enough to come and save her. Where are her parents? Why does no one believe her when she complains about her brother's behaviour?"

I explore this part with Claire's guidance and help the part feel heard and understood, cared about and safe.

I find myself telling Claire about the time when I was on stage at senior school. My mother had insisted I wore second-hand trousers handed down from a much slimmer second cousin. I shared the feeling of deep, deep shame I have felt for years whenever I think of that day. I say, "I stood on stage feeling awkward and very self-conscious. Instead of feeling proud of the achievements for which I was being recognised, I couldn't stop thinking that everyone must be looking at my thighs bulging against the fabric and stretching the seams. Then there was the sound of ripping and the feeling of terror as though the world was about to come crashing down on me."

Until sharing this aloud with Claire, I hadn't realised how much shame I have carried from that day when my trousers split in front of three hundred pupils and teachers, and how it has affected me ever since. The shame wasn't buried very deep. Although I have thought about this memory often, I hadn't known how to heal my inner child who experienced the shame. I have laughed about it as an adult, but my inner child has continued to feel this pain like it happened yesterday.

Claire helps me to get to know this ashamed part that is so sensitive to being stared at and feeling foolish. She helps me to befriend it and make it feel safe from further harm.

"No wonder I have palpitations every time I have to go on stage in my job," I say.

I share with Claire another time when my younger self felt shame for being stupid. She wasn't stupid, but she felt that she was.

I tell Claire, "Growing up, my older brother often teased me and on this occasion the effect was so strong that it has affected me for decades. My brothers were always made to help my dad in the garden and cleaning the cars, whilst I was made to stay indoors with my mum and help her clean the house. I wanted to be outside with the boys but was never given an option (one of the many reasons why I like autonomy today).

"Anyway, on this day my younger brother was on a Cubs camping trip and my dad said I could clean his car if I wanted to. My mum was in a foul mood with me and had told me to "get out of her sight" so I was free to go and help dad. I ran outside all excited to get started with the car and was feeling happy with myself and desperate to impress my dad. My older brother was washing mum's car and shouted over to me, 'I think you're going to need more elbow grease there, Sis.' I replied, 'Ah, okay thanks, where will I get that from?' My brother kept a poker face and shouted back, 'Try in the cleaning cupboard, under the kitchen sink.'

"I didn't stop to wonder why he was being unusually helpful. I ran into the kitchen and took everything out of the cupboard looking for the 'Elbow Grease'. Mum came into the kitchen, which she had just cleaned and screamed at me, 'What the hell are you doing, girl!' Sitting bolt upright on the floor I replied, "I'm trying to find the elbow grease.' My mum shouted again, 'Don't be stupid, Laura, there is no such thing as elbow grease!' I didn't stop there. 'Mark told me to come in here and get it.' I was defending myself, feeling wounded by her harsh tones. My mother shouted back at me, 'You're so easy to wind up, Laura. You need to grow up!'

"I don't remember finishing the car. I don't remember anything more about that memory, other than the feeling in my body every time I recall it. It is the same feeling I get whenever I think about doing something I may not be fully equipped to do. I feel my heart pound in my chest and my shoulders rise and crunch forward over my ribcage as though protecting my heart from bursting out of it. I feel my legs tingle as though wanting to run as fast as they can. If I allow myself to indulge in the memory, I can feel tears well in my eyes and my head pounds as I imagine beating my head against a wall for being so stupid and taking my brother's bait. I was about twelve years old. A time when we are already feeling vulnerable with all the hormonal changes going on in our bodies. I was teased for years by the whole family over and over again about this incident. They even told my boyfriends, thinking it too funny not to share."

There are so many memories that have haunted my inner child for years, until today. Claire helps me to unburden my inner child from the hurt caused all those years ago and carried into my adult years.

I tell Claire, "No wonder my protector parts have developed."

I know I will want to get to know my inner child and my protector parts more over time but for now I feel so much lighter already. I feel like now my inner child has been released from these feelings of hurt, my protector parts can take a step back. My inner child wants to have fun, to be silly, to dance, and to sing and laugh. My protector part that wants me to be so disciplined about food and exercise to avoid my inner child feeling the potential shame of ripping out of her clothes is going to take a step back. My HPS is sufficiently able to identify a more balanced approach to things. My HPS is also able to give me constructive criticism in a compassionate way if I don't get the balance right. My HPS is able to do this with curiosity and learn from any bad decisions, connecting with the feelings and emotions associated with them.

I can't wait to tell my friend Bridget about this experience. Bridget describes me as being so disciplined and serious that "I have a rod up my arse." She thinks I should let go and be more relaxed and sillier. I've always wanted to but had something (my inner child) stop me fully embracing a relaxed and silly me. Is it any wonder my inner child struggles to be silly? She's scared to laugh out loud.

I tell Claire, "One of my earliest memories is of being a child at nursery school and being told to stand outside the classroom because I had been laughing at something with Andrew Johnston. I was five years old, for goodness' sake! I felt shamed by this. I remember the pain of standing all alone in a cold hallway waiting to be asked to go back into the class and at the same time dreading the humiliation of having to walk through the sea of children to my desk in the far-right corner."

Claire helps me to find the part of me that felt the burden of this shame. Together we encourage her to let go of those feelings and to laugh as loud as she wants and to feel good about it.

Claire explains how laughing creates simple muscular exertions. She quotes Robin Dunbar, an evolutionary psychologist at Oxford:

"The simple muscular exertions involved in producing the familiar ha, ha, ha, ... trigger an increase in endorphins, the brain chemicals known for their feel-good effect."

Claire goes on to describe research studies that have demonstrated laughter's ability to reduce our physical pain.

I tell Claire, "It's all fascinating stuff. I feel I've been missing out on so much, and at the same time I'm excited to learn more and create more possibilities for myself. After all the stress I've experienced in life, my immune system is pretty damaged. I've read a lot about the impact of stress on our immune system from one of the books on your website."

"I want to boost my immune system and now that my inner child is happy to laugh more without feeling shame, bring on the fun times! Hopefully the 'feel-good' endorphins will also stop me craving the instant gratification of meaningless sex, sugar and wine."

Claire laughs with me. "Well, that's the idea!"

At the end of my session today, Claire explains that we can keep coming back to parts of me throughout the coaching as and when they appear, and I want to get to know them better to help me be my HPS more often. In the meantime, our next session is going to be focused on some techniques for boosting my superpowers. Wow, I can't wait!

Self-care Checklist

[3]Claire has sent me a Self-care Checklist to use regularly to help me connect with myself and find out what I may need more of in order to access my HPS more quickly and easily and maintain this state for longer. She suggests I schedule a time every week to do this. I have decided to do the review every Sunday evening as part of my reflection activity.

The Benefits of Laughter

She has given me a few links to more articles that include research on the benefits of laughter and how to laugh more. I'm definitely reading these:

https://provine.umbc.edu/books/laughter-a-scientific-investigation/

https://www.psychologytoday.com/intl/articles/199607/happily-ever-laughter

https://thethirty.whowhatwear.com/what-happens-to-your-brain-when-you-laugh

Claire suggests I continue to complete my evening ritual of the 'Daily Reflection Activity' as before and add in reflections on what I do that makes me laugh, how this feels and what impact it has on my mood and performance outcomes.

Journal, Day 120

I went to stay with Bridget this weekend. There is no better friend to make me laugh than good old Bridget. Bridget makes a joke out of almost anything and everything and I love her dearly for it. After she put the kids to bed we opened a bottle of red wine and started reliving some of our dating stories. Between us we have quite a few. Once we were on the second bottle of wine we decided to have a look at what men were on offer on Match.com.

Bridget's profile was already on the site. So, we sat side by side on the sofa, drinking and judging all the poor men. I'm not proud of our judgemental behaviour, but at the same time it was so funny. There were so many men we would just dismiss, saying things like, "How rude, he winked at me," and "He's awful, can't he see I'm too good for him?" and "Ugly!", "Vile", "Too Old", "Too Fat", "Too Thin", "Too Short". We were so awful about them and we laughed out loud like I only ever do with Bridget. Afterwards we crossed our bodies and apologised to God for our outrageous behaviour and then laughed again.

Bridget had to rush to the bathroom after laughing so much she wet herself; even her Tena Lady couldn't cope. This made me laugh more. Thank God, I have been doing my pelvic floor exercises. I wish there was a better alternative to online dating but, sadly, meeting a man any other way just doesn't seem to happen these days. The evening of laughter did me the world of good and reminded me to read up on the links Claire sent me.

I read the articles and the research on the benefits of laughter. Here are a few things I picked up that particularly resonated with me:

According to humour guru William Fry, Professor Emeritus of Psychiatry at Stanford University:

"Laughter also increases production of immunity-boosting gamma interferon and speeds up the production of new immune cells. And it reduces levels of the stress hormone cortisol, which can weaken the immune response."

He also writes that...

"Creativity and humour are identical... They both involve bringing together two items which do not have an obvious connection and creating a relationship."

I have never been that creative. This could be one of the reasons why:

"Fry found that by the time the average kid reaches kindergarten, he or she is laughing some 300 times each day. Compare that to the typical adult...who laughs a paltry seventeen times a day."

After the shame of being sent outside the class when I was about five, I wasn't your typical kindergarten child. I think I probably laughed a lot less than three hundred times a day, even then. I bet lots of kids get the laughter shamed out of them, whilst life also becomes way too serious. What a real shame that is!

I've been reflecting on shame since my last session with Claire. I noticed another book on her website she recommends. *Dare to Lead* by Brené Brown. Brené is an American professor, lecturer, author, and podcast host. She started her career as a 'shame researcher' and is now the author of numerous best-selling books. She is fascinating, as is her research on courage, vulnerability, shame and empathy. I've ordered all of her books: *The Gifts of Imperfection, Daring Greatly, Rising Strong, Braving the Wilderness and Dare to Lead*. I've started with *Dare to Lead* as I am keen to reflect on how some of my protector parts may have influenced some of my leadership behaviour at work.

My first thoughts are that I have been much more of a defensive leader than was helpful and this probably manifests itself in a degree of perfectionism - unrealistic high expectations, working too hard, expecting others to do the same. I can be a bit overly challenging and assert my power when I get triggered. Alongside this, I know I often do things for approval even if they don't necessarily add value. This is definitely worth working through further. I wonder sometimes how I have been so successful whilst having all these aspects of me that work against me.

In the William Fry article, he recommends a two-step process for people who want to inoculate themselves with laughter.

1. First, figure out your humour profile.

- Listen to yourself for a few days and see what makes you laugh out loud. Be honest with yourself; don't affect a taste for sophisticated French farces if your heartiest guffaws come from watching Moe, Larry, and Curly. (I'm guessing these are the American version of The Chuckle Brothers.)

For me, this is definitely Bridget, Abi (her laugh is so infectious) and observational comedy such as Jason Manford, Chris Ramsey and the 'garlic bread' guy, Peter Kay. I also like laughing at myself when I do daft things. I'm quite clumsy and often walk into glass doors and lamp posts and spill my food down my top. Abi thinks this is hilarious as I pride myself on being so smart and in control and then do daft things like these.

2. Next, he says, use your comic profile to start building your own humour library: books, magazines, videos, what have you.

- If possible, set aside a portion of your bedroom or den as a "humour corner" to house your collection.
- Then, when life gets you down, don't hesitate to visit.

I love this idea. I'm going to add some of my favourite comedians to my social media and look up some of their stuff on Netflix and Prime and schedule one each weekend to top up my laughter meter. Bridget lives hours away so I can't go and see her every weekend for my weekly top up of laughter. We have agreed to do virtual Zoom & Wine calls more often though. (Just not too much wine.)

Here's today's six-minute reflection:

Daily Reflection Activity

3 minutes

Write whatever comes to mind when reflecting on the day.

I'm in a great mood. It must be the serotonin after all the recent laughing. I am loving this journey of learning and self-improvement.

I'm a bit addicted. Claire said the buzz we get from learning something new generates dopamine and dopamine is addictive, so I just want to learn more. It's much healthier than an alcohol and sugar addiction. I want it to make me a better person and a better leader. Maybe I will achieve that global role and the house on the beach I imagined in my Ideal Future, not to mention the tall dark stranger I envisaged stood on the deck of the house.

I loved my weekend with Bridget. We laughed so much my belly ached. I feel like I have pulled muscles in and around my stomach and rib cage. That reminds me, I really must do some more core exercises and Pilates.

We had a few too many wines last night. Now I'm nursing a hangover I wish I didn't have, as there is so much I want to read and learn. At least this time, I wasn't drinking because I was trying to numb my feelings. I've stopped doing that lately. I was just going with the flow, literally. And it felt good not to be overthinking. It felt good to be at ease.

Unfortunately, the hangover has influenced my food decisions today. Driving back from Bridget's I ate a McDonalds breakfast muffin with hash brown and then called into Tesco and bought a packet of custard creams which I have demolished on the sofa whilst devouring my new Brené Brown book. I'm shattered now so my original plan to even out the weekend calories with a big session at the gym are out of the window.

2 minutes

Read what you wrote and write what insights you get from this.

Too much alcohol leads to bad food and no exercise and I feel unhappy with this situation.

I didn't need the alcohol to have fun with Bridget, of this I am sure. I just need to learn to set a limit and stick to it.

I love learning. I forgot how much I love learning. I used to read so much as a child and then having children and a career got in the way. Whilst I have gained amazing learning through experience, there is just so much more to learn. Learning energises me and I like that.

1 minute

Read what insights you wrote and decide if you want to take action as a result. Write down what actions you want to take.

I am going to schedule time for my reading so that I can make it part of my routine and not allow other things in life and work to get in the way. I have read an article recently that said something along the lines of 'leaders are readers'. I guess I can keep learning and perhaps start to share some of what I learn with others. I might start a book club within my team at work.

Journal, Day 122 - Coaching session with Claire

We meet at the hotel in York again. The session starts in the usual way and I share with Claire my progress. I tell her I feel like I am understanding my parts better and I am managing to notice when one becomes hurt or protective and I use my 'Notice, Movement, Mood, New Posture, Mantra' sequence to separate my HPS from my part.

Claire reminds me, "At the same time, make sure you acknowledge your part for being there for you and let it know 'I've got this'. If your parts feel you have forgotten about them or you are ignoring them or blaming them, they will not be happy and will let you know they want attention by blending with you."

Claire suggests I think about my parts as my 'inner team'. At work I wouldn't ignore, blame or get annoyed at my team (well, not deliberately). Let's say one of my team showed up for something and I didn't think I needed them for it. I would always consider first if this team member could be of value. If not, I would show my gratitude and thank them whilst politely standing them down. Well, at least my HPS would treat the situation like this. This makes total sense to me.

Today, Claire asks me if I would like to learn some extra simple things I can do to further develop the superpowers of my HPS. Of course, I would. I'm excited to add some tools to my toolkit. It's like I'm on a journey to creating a 'Super Neuro Me', like in my mantra.

Claire calls this **Superpower Boosts!** I love it.

Claire says, "Laura, in one of our previous sessions you said you wanted to find more purpose in your life, just like Wonder Woman. Is this still the case?" Claire remembers everything!

I say, "Yes, I do. I feel as though my purpose has been to survive through the past few decades rather than thrive. I want to thrive now and as part of that I feel as though I need more meaning in my life. I want my life to mean something. Does that sound daft? Abi was a big part of why I did what I have done in the past. I have always wanted to be a good role model for her, although I'm not convinced I always did a good job.

"Over the past few months, I have realised I was driven at work based on a survival instinct. My wounded 'inner child' didn't feel good enough. She felt it necessary to work hard to prove herself to people and a lot of the time that wasn't necessary. Now, I can see how many of my drivers were unhealthy. I don't want this to be what I role model to Abi."

Claire asks, "Laura, what is it about Wonder Woman that made you think you wanted more purpose in your life?"

"I respect her focus on something bigger than her. I feel like I pay way too much attention to me, in a way that is unhealthy. Yes, I want to work on developing myself, but outside of that I want to think more about other people and the world at large. I spend way too much time looking in the mirror and obsessing about fine lines or grey hairs, or the numbers on the scales, or the number of calories in a bagel, or the number of calories I've burned at a spinning class. Do you know what I mean, Claire?'

"I certainly do. I've been there. Remembering what I used to be like makes me feel a little stressed. All that attention on things that don't really matter but you're allowing them to matter way too much. Does this make you feel stressed too, Laura?"

"It does; it's crazy!"

"In that case, let's get started on your Purpose."

Purpose

[1]As we worked through the session on purpose, this is, in brief, what I came up with.

Step One: Consider what you are deeply passionate about

What is it that matters to you most of all? Try to list up to six things.

Think about things you love: what do you love doing so much you lose track of time? What do you spend your free time doing? What do you prioritise money for? What makes you feel your most authentic you?

- *Abi*
- *My health*
- *Helping others, my friends and my colleagues, having strong relationships*
- *Learning and being creative*

- *Having a laugh*
- *Living in the present*

Great, now what is not important to you? (Try to list up to six things.)

Perhaps consider, what didn't feature in your Vision of Success? What did you need to let go of to achieve your Vision of Success?

- *Status*
- *I don't remember thinking what size or weight I was, just that I was fit and healthy*
- *Being independent: there was a significant man in my future*
- *Being perfect: there was sand on the floor of my home and I wasn't irritated by that*
- *Being right – knowing everything*
- *Holding on to the past, regretting, blaming, ruminating*

Step Two: Consider what the world needs

What do you consider an important world issue that needs the attention of more people?

- *Young girls need better role models*
- *The next generation need to be better at making the world a better place*
- *We need the corporate balance sheet to account for its impact on the human race*

Step Three: Consider your unique contribution

What are your greatest strengths?

- *I can command a room, engage the attention of people*
- *I have a large network of contacts and I'm very good at connecting them in support of each other*
- *I can be like a dog with a bone when I want something enough*
- *I'm a brilliant negotiator, always able to find a win/win*
- *I know my industry sector very well*
- *I'm old enough to have some wisdom and young enough to have lots of energy still to apply it*

Step Four: Consider your ideal life

How can you apply your unique contribution to what you are passionate about and what the world needs whilst creating the lifestyle you want?

- *There is a theme running through this about relationships.*
- *A theme about health.*
- *There is something about my influencing/negotiating skills.*
- *Perhaps I could use my role at 'Health Foods' to give me a platform to bring people from the Health Food sector together to do more than just sell Health Foods. We can sell Health Foods and run the company in a way that promotes better mental and physical health. We can look at every aspect of how we do business individually and collectively and change it to encourage and reinforce positive health.*
- *We could be the forerunners for other companies to follow. We could demonstrate how making a positive impact on health in the way we do business positively impacts the bottom line. This is the win/win I'm always looking for.*
- *We will need to be creative and find new ways to do things, like using different models and sponsors for our products. We will need to have people advising us on how what we do now has a positive and negative impact on health. We will have to get the accounting people to look at how we account for things differently. I love it.*
- *It won't be easy convincing people to begin with, but that's what I love doing, convincing people of a different way to do things.*

Step Five: Do you want this to be your legacy? (If not, think again.)

- *Thinking about this makes me feel tingly all over.*
- *I feel like all my cells are bouncing around in my body with excitement!*
- *I can do this. It will be challenging but I can do this.*
- *This will be worthwhile. This is Wonder Woman territory and I want to play!*

Step Six: Do your Purpose and Vision for the future align?

- *They absolutely do.*
- *They align perfectly.*
- *I can see myself being happier and healthier and achieving more at work and being recognised more with this clarity of purpose driving me.*

The coaching session with Claire is brilliant. I feel so energised just working through the steps to get to my purpose, that it bodes well for doing the work to achieve it.

Claire is right, this is a superpower boost.

Before we leave the session, Claire walks me through three more superpower boost exercises to do as homework. She also reminds me to continue with my mindfulness exercises, noticing how my body feels and responding effectively to regulate when starting to dysregulate and completing my daily reflection. These are all ways to maintain my superpowers.

My Homework

From Vision and Purpose to Goals

[2]These are my take-aways from the conversation with Claire about goals. Above all else, goals should be meaningful to you. Lots of people create goals which are trendy or seasonal. Take New Year Resolutions, for example. Most people set resolutions to drink less alcohol, eat less sugar, exercise more and so on. Goals set because it's seasonal to do so are a little forced, and humans resist force.

The second issue with these goals is that they originate from a negative place: 'I've drunk, eaten and sat on the sofa watching movies too much over Christmas and therefore I must do these things to compensate or rectify a problem.' Having a goal like this isn't going to motivate you to do what you need to do to achieve an outcome. In fact, there is no real measurable outcome in these goals.

Your goals need to be YOUR goals. Not you following the crowd. They are there to help you achieve your Vision and Purpose, so that's your starting point.

What goals will you need to achieve to fulfil your Vision and Purpose?

In my Vision I saw myself working in a global role, with more of an emphasis on brand value, inspiring future leaders and being a role model for health-based Values.

To achieve this, I will need to:

1. *Improve my global leadership skills – I've never worked globally before. I will need to be able to flex my style to working with people from different cultures. I need to find a course specifically on this and a mentor who already has a global role and is seen as a role model in global leadership skills.*

2. *Improve my visibility within the organisation's global hierarchy. Maybe this is where I channel my purpose to sell Health Foods and run the company in a way that promotes better mental and physical health. OMG this is brilliant. I need to get my boss and my peers on board with this idea*

and see if I can create a coalition, with my boss sponsoring
what we do. I will aim to have everyone on board by the
end of the year. It will take years to make it happen but
getting them on board is the start. How exciting!

3. *I really want to change the way I work so that I can show*
others how we can all work in a healthier way. I want this
more than anything. I want this for me and for others and I
want it to be sustainable. I feel I am on the journey with
this through the coaching so far with Claire. I need some
form of measure, though. I need to know I have achieved it.
It's not about my weight or how many burpees I can do. It's
more about how I feel. I want to feel healthy. I want to eat
a balanced diet, exercise regularly, drink alcohol in
moderation, sleep well, have time for rest, time for friends
and family, and time in nature.

4. *In my vision I saw a man in my house. I would like to meet*
a man. At this point, though, this is not an immediate goal.
I would rather meet a man when goal three is more
established.

5. *I have good working relationships with people at work but*
in my vision everyone, including me, was so much more
relaxed. We were smiling and laughing more. We were
working more collaboratively and being more creative. If
this is what I want, what can I do to achieve this? The
work I am doing with Claire to be more of my Highest
Potential Self will surely help me relate better to others and
not just to my 'inner team'. Maybe my goal on this is to
achieve scores of five against each of the superpowers of

HPS when I reflect at the end of each week. Or is that me doing my perfectionist thing again? Okay, there are nine superpowers and each has a highest possible score of five. That's 45 in total. I would like to score at least 40/45 at the end of each week. I would like to be able to do this consistently twelve months from now.

6. *I want to have a stronger, deeper connection with a small number of friends in my vision. I will make sure I make time for this as I plan my schedule. I don't want to get so wrapped up in my career that I ignore my friends. I also want to open up to them more. I have been doing this more lately and I want it to continue. I will make spending regular quality time with my main friends such as Bridget, Louise and Cheryl a goal. I will spend at least a couple of weekends with each of them a year doing something fun and having meaningful conversations where we really open up to each other rather than just catch up.*

I know I will need to smarten these goals further, but I think I have made a good start. They feel integrated and they all depend upon me maintaining my HPS. I will share them with Claire at our next coaching session.

Power up your home environment

[3]Claire briefs me to reflect upon my home environment to see what might need to change to help me be more at ease and at the same time stay focused. Claire explains, "Our minds can only focus on so much at once. We have control over our home environment. We can make this help us to focus on things that are aligned to how we want to feel, which increases the chance of us feeling those feelings."

It makes perfect sense. Claire suggests that clutter specifically is a distraction.

"Visually, there's always something to take your focus away from the task at hand. Practically speaking, you'll spend valuable time looking for items that you need (rather than completing the tasks on your plate). It can also increase stress. Accounting for the emotional baggage all your various belongings bring with them can be mentally exhausting."

As always, Claire offers me some reading on the subject.

https://www.nytimes.com/2019/01/03/well/mind/clutter-stress-procrastination-psychology.html

I have a few things to consider:

What will prompt me to relax more effectively?

- *I decide to move my phone out of my bedroom at night and charge it in my dressing room.*
- *I will keep all my work-related books in my office, leaving shelf space in the lounge and my bedroom for self-improvement and fiction.*
- *I will buy one of those bath shelves for across the bath and put candles on it. I will double the number of candles and infusers around the room. These extra fragrances will help to boost my mood. Candlelight rather than electric lighting will also make me more relaxed in the evening and ready for bed at a sensible time.*
- *I will also declutter. I have way too much stuff from the past. I need to make room for things I can associate with the new me. I will spend this weekend having a good clear out.*

What will keep you focused on your Vision and Purpose?

- *I am going to recreate my Vision on a Vision Board using a collage of pictures from magazines and some bright bold pens. I will also do something creative with my purpose and put both of these into frames and hang them side by side in my kitchen so that I can keep a constant reminder of where I am going.*

- *Once I have decluttered and removed the 'old me' from the house I will look for new things to help me stay focused on the new me. I am going to buy an ornamental globe to keep me focused on the global agenda of my purpose and the global role. I am going to bring more music into the house by having a music system in my lounge and speakers in rooms throughout the house. This way I can bring more life and energy and buzz into the house when I want it. I might even dance in my pants throughout the house, just for fun!*

- *I am going to go through my kitchen cupboards, throw out unhealthy food, and pop the few bottles of alcohol in the garage (out of sight, out of mind). If I really want something unhealthy, I can pop to the shops for it. If I really want a glass of wine or a gin I can go into the garage for a bottle. There is no need to have temptation staring me in the face every time I put the kettle on.*

Power up your wardrobe

[4]This is similar to the home environment exercise.

Claire suggests I declutter my wardrobe.

Use separate boxes for charity, Abi and rubbish.

Take everything out of one wardrobe, drawer and cupboard at a time.

Lay everything on the bed.

Clean the wardrobe, cupboard or drawer.

For each item, decide whether it is going to help you feel more at ease or more fit and healthy.

Is it going to make you feel happy?

Is it going to make you feel like the you in your vision of your future?

If the answer is no, choose an appropriate box to pop it in and go on to the next item.

If the answer is yes, pop it back into the wardrobe, cupboard or drawer.

Claire suggests when I have finished this exercise I will be ready to make a list of anything I feel is missing.

She recommends I read a few articles if I want to know more about it. She tells me the gist: "There's a phenomenon that scientists have dubbed 'enclothed cognition'. This is simply the scientific term for the idea that clothing impacts how we think. The theory says that what we wear (or what others are wearing) actually changes our thought patterns. In our history, for centuries dress was the number one status symbol. It told people where you ranked in society, how much you could afford, and what your profession was. Certain colours (like purple) and fabrics (like silk) were reserved for the royal or elite classes. Years ago, the working class would save up to buy a purple dress or accessory to try to improve their status."

I suppose it is still a little like this today. Clothes have become an engrained part of our society. What you wear signals to others who you are and where you belong in this world.

Claire says, "More importantly, it sends a signal to your own brain about how it feels to be dressed, what kind of thoughts it needs to possess and how it needs to behave while wearing that kind of outfit."

I ask Claire if there is any research to back this up, and she says, "I know of a study using doctors' lab coats. In the first part of the study, half of the participants were given lab coats and the other half remained in their own clothes. Those dressed in white coats made fewer mistakes and focused better than those in their own clothes.

"In the second half of the experiment, they gave everyone the same coats, but they told half it was a doctor's coat and half it was a protective coat for a painter. Those who thought it was a doctor's coat could again focus harder and longer than those in the painter's coat.

"Researchers suggested that this was because doctors are known to be attentive and detail-oriented, so those in the lab coats began to take on similar 'doctor' traits."

Typically, Claire gives the final word on the matter to Wonder Woman and her superhero pals.

"Why do you think it is so important for Wonder Woman, Batman, Spiderman and the rest to have a costume instead of dressing like their alter ego? Let's face it, Clark Kent and Superman look exactly the same, just wearing different outfits. Clark wears glasses and a badly fitting suit to denote he is a nerdy journalist and when he turns into Superman he has a lycra body suit to show off his bulging muscles, to remind him and us that he is physically and emotionally strong. The outfit hardly acts as a disguise. It is much more about how it makes him feel."

I reply, "It's the same for Wonder Woman. She doesn't even have a mask to hide her face as Wonder Woman. It is blatantly obvious that Diana Prince and Wonder Woman are the same person."

"Exactly, Laura. However, Diana wears her hair and her clothes conservatively to represent her as an ever so intelligent, hard-working, introverted character throughout her evolution from army nurse, to naval officer, to businesswoman. She is often seen wearing a uniform in her roles as many of us do in everyday life. Even if it is not a formal uniform, we wear something that denotes what we are doing and how we need to feel to do that job."

I want my clothes to remind me that I am comfortable, not trying too hard, not distracted by high heels that hurt my feet and not getting a sore back because I'm trying to hold in my core in a body con dress. I want to feel comfortable yet still smart, showing an effort in my appearance without it being too much of an effort. I want to be dressed warmly enough and with flat shoes to go for a walk when I'm in the office. I want to have a little bit of edge, though, to remind myself about my creativity, just a little something that stops me being boring and makes me smile each day.

I share with Claire, "I'm excited to sort out my Super Neuro Me' wardrobe!"

Journal, Day 140

I have had such fun over the last few weeks making my Vision and Purpose Boards and getting them framed. Just doing this has further embedded my commitment to them. I have also sorted out my wardrobe and given my whole house a spring clean and boosted every space with elements of the new me. Every day I feel so much clearer and calmer and more creative, just being in my house. I am going to do what I can in my office and encourage my team to do the same to our entire workspace.

I have another coaching session with Claire today. It's just an hour online to see how I am getting on with my super-power boosts and to offer me a few more. I'm really feeling in the zone. People at work are commenting on my good mood. Was I in such a bad mood before?

I have found myself being so much more at ease lately, asking more questions of others and listening more to their ideas rather than feeling the need to be in charge and domi-nate with my views. My team have made some fantastic changes to the office and they are loving my invitation to them to bring more of their true self to work.

I haven't been focusing so much on my weight and the calories I'm consuming yet I feel lighter, slimmer and my clothes feel less tight and uncomfortable on me. I have bought some new clothes too and I've tended to go for slightly more colourful clothes, simple, stylish, flattering but comfortable. I've bought smart jeans for work and elegant but flat long boots. I feel great in these with a range of new tops. I can just pull on a jacket or coat and go for a walk at lunchtime.

I've been inviting members of the team out for a walk and talk at lunchtime. It saves time, we have a great conversation, have fresh air and exercise and go back to the office together to eat our lunch whilst finishing our conversation. It feels like the variety and casualness of this improve our conversation as so many more good ideas come out of them and I feel we are sharing more feedback with each other too. It's really making a difference. I feel like I'm on a bit of a roll.

Coaching session

I'm eager to share my progress with Claire and equally eager to find out more about what I can do to keep on this positive path.

Claire says, "That all sounds fantastic, Laura. I'm so pleased for you. It sounds as though you are enjoying implementing your superpower boosts and that they are starting to make a difference too."

She seems genuinely chuffed for me. I'm waiting for the 'but' and the pause and something negative. I'm still a little cynical after 'Fuckwit'. Life is definitely getting a lot better, but I thought life was great in the beginning with him and then look what happened. I was deceived, lulled into a false sense of security and given hope for a better life. Then within months it all unravelled and in the first few weeks after we separated I felt so low. I didn't know who I could trust, and I didn't even know if I could trust myself. It's only been a matter of months and things seem to be so much better. I am trusting Claire and I am feeling much more optimistic about my future. I share my thoughts with Claire.

Build your Tribe

Claire responds, "Laura, you've achieved a lot over the past few months. You've worked really hard at being vulnerable and open and at trying things. You've been amazing. It is critical to a happy life to accept there will be ups and downs. I cannot guarantee that the rest of your life will be plain sailing and you can't control that either. What is most important is that you have the basics in place to bring your HPS to the situation. And even in doing this you have to be prepared to sometimes need a little help.

"How would you like today to work on your support system? Perhaps if you have more confidence in the support system around you, you will be less concerned about what happens when you hit a bump in the road."

That sounds great to me. I have always had plenty of people around me, but rarely have I been good at leaning on them when I needed to. My upbringing made me so independent, I couldn't lean on my first husband and when I finally trusted enough to marry again, husband number two turned out not to be trustworthy. I have tended to have friends who needed me, and I have supported them. I haven't really had people I felt I could be vulnerable with and be the one asking for help. I share my thoughts with Claire.

She answers, "This is important because your support system needs to be reciprocal. Think of them as your tribe. Tribe members are people who accept you just as you are. They support you through difficult times in your life, provide you with a sense of community and encourage you to pursue your dreams."

Claire speaks with such sincerity. I believe her and I get a sense she has her own tribe supporting her, keeping her so calm and confident and reassuring. After all, I know her life has had its ups and downs too. Claire will often share with me when she can relate to me from personal experience. She is able to empathise and connect with me, without making it about her.

"Laura, you may be aware that secure attachment is a basic human need from an early age. Humans possess an intrinsic tribal mentality inherited from our ancestors. In the early evolution of man, safety in numbers provided protection from danger, pooling resources assisted in times of scarcity, while shared knowledge increased the chance of survival. It's not that different today. Positive social connection promotes happiness. Surrounding yourself with people who show you genuine care and understanding can encourage you to be authentic and will bring out your HPS."

It makes sense and I guess I knew this already, but I hadn't really slowed down enough to think about it or considered what it means for me. When facing a challenging time such as relationship problems, difficulties at work, redundancy, illness or stress, I would keep myself to myself. I learnt during my childhood it is better to do this, otherwise you are just seen as another problem to add to mum and dad's list of problems. I can see how connecting with like-minded individuals can not only provide support and guidance but may also open new networks and opportunities. It just never really occurred to me to try.

Claire went on to share some of the neuroscience of social connection. "Social connectivity triggers the release of the feel-good hormone, oxytocin, which in turn triggers the release of serotonin. Serotonin activates a region in your brain central to your reward system. You may remember that serotonin results in feelings of happiness. Because of this link to the reward system, social interaction becomes something desirable."

"So, I've been missing out on serotonin, especially when I needed it."

Claire gives me a look of sympathy and I hear her release a little sigh of empathy. I wonder how many other people she sees who have been missing out on what is freely available.

She says, "Not just serotonin but oxytocin too. You have been missing out on the opportunity of both neurotransmitter hormones. Oxytocin has been identified as an important neurochemical that allows the body to adapt to highly emotive situations. It encourages relaxation, trust and a sense of psychological stability. In turn this enables more effective cognitive function and social and emotional behaviour.

"You are much happier in yourself these days. We need to make sure you have the right people around you to encourage that to continue."

I feel a bit foolish, but I get over this and come straight out and ask Claire how I go about finding my tribe.

Claire answers, "I've mentioned Brené Brown before. She also writes about finding your tribe. It's worth reading some of her work on this. She writes about the importance of authenticity. You have to show up as your imperfect and vulnerable self.

"At the same time, you need to be emotionally equipped to assist other members of your tribe to achieve their aspirations. You at you HPS will show up with the qualities necessary to be an effective tribe member. Your tribe may include people interested in a similar purpose to you and also people with the same core values."

I've done lots of work over the years on brand values and corporate values, but oddly I haven't really considered my own values that deeply. Claire explains the process to understand my values is similar to what we did when considering my purpose and is worth doing some home-work on it to help me bottom out my 'Core Values', the non-negotiables.

"The thing is, Laura, you don't want everyone in your tribe to be the same as you. Where would be the fun in that? Also, you wouldn't learn much from a tribe that all had the same beliefs, thought the same, had the same life experiences and wanted exactly the same things. However, there will be some core values that will be important for you to feel you can be yourself and be vulnerable with each other. This is what you need to focus on."

Claire sits back in her chair and sips on her coffee. This encourages me to take more time to think. She says, "Finding your tribe means connecting with people who tell you what you **need** to hear, as opposed to what you **want to hear**, but do it constructively and without judgement. By showing up with your tribe as your HPS you can come from a place of non-judgement. You will be using your superpowers, particularly curiosity, compassion and connectedness.

"It's important to understand the traits and qualities you value in other members of your tribe. It's also worthwhile connecting with people who inspire you.

According to group contagion theory, we model the behaviour of those around us. Can you give me an example of a behaviour you would want others in your tribe to have?"

I think for a while. One of the most obvious things in my vision is a healthy me. I would want people in my tribe to be interested in being healthy and to role model this, to keep me on track. I share this with Claire.

She says, "Research has proven that happiness is contagious. A range of studies conducted by sociology professors James Fowler and Nicholas Christakis clearly show that the health and wellbeing of one person affects the health and wellbeing of others in the same social networks. Christakis and Fowler have explored the idea that emotions are a collective phenomenon. Their studies demonstrate how happiness can spread through social networks from one individual to another in a chain reaction. Happiness and health go together. Laura, can you see how critical it is to choose members of your tribe wisely? Think of it like Wonder Woman deciding to join the Justice League."

Claire sits back, smiles at me and has another sip of her latte. I think for a while then reply.

"I love the idea of being part of an inspirational support group. I've not really been much of a group person before. I have been a leader of work teams but not part of a social group before. This could be interesting for me."

"I agree. Finding your tribe will help you to practise your HPS in a safe environment and have people encourage you to be more of your HPS. Your tribe will encourage you to be authentic. They will provide you with the support and encouragement to have the confidence to feel enough as you currently are."

"Yes, it will be good for me to practise more vulnerability outside work to begin with whilst developing the courage to be myself more at work."

Claire fidgets a little, which is unusual. I wait, intrigued to hear what she is about to say. "Laura, I wouldn't rule out finding your tribe at work, even initially. They may not be in your immediate peer group, but they are very likely to be there, otherwise your workplace is probably the wrong place for you to work. I haven't got that impression before."

Now it is my turn to fidget, and I think for a while. "I've worked elsewhere where I was much less comfortable being myself. I think I can be more authentic here. I was imagining opening up about my feelings at work and this would be new to people. I'm worried it might unnerve them."

Claire suggests I start small and build over time, but don't rule out making shifts at work, which is good advice.

"One other thing. It's helpful to remember that everyone has strengths and weaknesses and unique characteristics, so whilst you are looking for mutual core values, a degree of tolerance and appreciation for individual differences continues to be important."

That's a good point. I need and like to be challenged and I value diversity to help me grow. It's particularly important given my ambitions for a global role in the future. When Claire could see I had stopped thinking through her last sentence to me, she went on to say, "The research into the spread of happiness via social networks also demonstrates that it's not the size of your tribe that brings about greater happiness. Happiness is based on the number of positive connections you create within your tribe. So, a small group of people who you positively connect with is the key."

At the end of another insightful session, we finish with my homework for the next few weeks.

My Homework

Core Values

[5]Claire suggests I follow the 'Identify Your Personal Values' Workbook on her website to identify my values before I start to find people with similar values to be part of my tribe.

Superpower morning routine

[6]You are more likely to have a good day if you take a positive action first thing in the morning (provided this does not involve being on a screen such as your TV, phone, tablet or laptop).

for example:

- Refresh in a cold shower.
- Drink a glass of water.
- Set your intentions for the day.
- Move – five mins cardio, five mins stretching, five mins tidying, five mins dancing whilst the kettle brews.
- Write down five things you are grateful for.
- Stand in front of a mirror and smile. Tell yourself 'I am so looking forward to today'.
- Give your significant other and/or children a heartfelt hug and tell them you love them.
- Meditate.
- Reflect in your Journal.
- Learn something - read a book, listen to a podcast.
- Tackle your hardest task of the day and feel accomplished.
- **Or do all of the above!**

Identify your superpower morning routine. Take inspiration from this list but don't be wedded to it. Try it! Reflect on how it makes you feel and how it changes what you achieve each day. Write up your reflections in your journal.

Journal, Day 170

What a lovely few days with Abi. I loved the Lake District and absolutely will go more often. There are so many lovely walks and I just love the feeling I get when I am there. It is so relaxing and the views are stunning. We walked each day despite the persistent rain.

On our first day, we met with my cousin and her son for lunch in Grasmere. Poor Nathan was very shy and probably couldn't wait to be on his own again with his mum instead of listening to three women talking what he probably thought was a load of rubbish. We loved talking rubbish, though. We had a good laugh in the café. You can't have too much of a good laugh. The biggest laugh came when I saw a picture of a cow on the wall and pointed it out to the girls and said, "That's nice but I prefer the udder one" then I looked in the opposite direction. Abi caught on to the joke, but my cousin didn't get it. She kept asking, "What other one?" We couldn't stop laughing long enough to tell her it was a joke. By the time we had got over ourselves and explained, we realised it wasn't that funny after all. By this time my stomach muscles ached from laughing so much.

There has always been something infectious about Abi's laugh. She looks so beautiful when she laughs whereas I'm convinced I have an ugly laughing face. It is almost as bad as my ugly crying face. Also, Abi laughs so innocently and freely it's heart-warming. There is little I enjoy more than laughing with my daughter.

Our B&B was ok. It was not as nice as advertised and the owner was a bit standoffish. The breakfast, however, was delicious, although the seats were uncomfortable. I hate sitting on uncomfortable seats. When looking for a bar, café or restaurant I always look for comfy seats! They had good Wi-Fi, which was great as we were in bed early every night. Thankfully, we could download Netflix and BBC iPlayer and watch movies in bed.

We had a stunning walk over the hills behind Lake Windermere on Saturday. We combined this with a potter around the villages of Windermere and Bowness, a few café stops, and a glass of wine outside a bar in Windermere. I know I said I was cutting down on the booze and I meant what I said. I said I would only have a drink when I really wanted one and I really wanted one.

I didn't think we had gone over the top whilst away, though. Most days we averaged more than 3000 calories burned, as registered on my Fitbit. I didn't feel we ate more than 3000 each day but I have come back two pounds heavier. I feel like Bridget Jones constantly going on about my weight. It obviously really bugs me on the one hand and on the other I think, "Look, I'm not that bad. In fact, I look pretty good." I just want to feel better and losing the extra half a stone I am carrying would make me feel so much better; it always does.

I've decided to take on a personal trainer. Perhaps spending the time and money on that will help me stay disciplined. It isn't my meals that are the problem as I am very good with those and I eat a salad most of the time. It's not alcohol as I don't drink that often. It is the snacking and lattes! This week it was chocolate! I must stop. I want to stop. I haven't got any chocolate at home after my clear out. I've probably just made the most of being away. It doesn't feel good though. I need to drink more water as I have been having a lot of headaches recently. It's probably all the caffeine in the coffees and the chocolate. No wonder I have felt tired.

I have my trip to see Colleen in Zurich next weekend too and I must be good. I am going to be brave and tell her I have stopped drinking to avoid her encouraging me to have one. I am going to only have the odd glass of wine when I really want it from now on and not when people are making me drink with them to make them feel better. I have noticed this happens. I am being good with my food and not drinking and it is other people who say things like, "Don't be silly, live a little." I think they say this to make themselves feel better about what they are eating and drinking, and I stupidly let them influence me. Well, not anymore.

Anyway, back to our trip. One of my worst bad food days in the Lakes was when we invited my Dad and Dawn over. We had walked on our own in the morning, just a few miles but great views. We met Dad and Dawn in what had become our favourite place, "Café Italia".

After lunch, we had another walk with them down to the boatyard. We hired a boat which was supposed to be a 'premium' boat. There was not a lot of premium about it but nonetheless everyone seemed excited to get on board. The best laugh turned out to be getting on and off the boat. We had the canopy on because of the rain so we had to crawl in over the driver's seat. It was okay for me and Abi and a bit more of a struggle for the 'Oldies' but it provided plenty of laughs, especially watching poor Dad. Dad drove the boat for the first half then Abi took over. I don't think they could see much for the rain pouring down on the window but thankfully there weren't many boats out because of the wet weather.

We shared one of our Easter eggs and I had bought mini bottles of Cava for us to drink with straws. We took photos and chatted and the two hours I had hired the boat for flew by. Dad and Dawn left about sixish. I loved seeing Dad with Abi; she only really has him as a strong male role model. I also love seeing my Dad with his girls. He seems so happy, it makes my heart sing with joy. I can feel it now as I remember the day.

Monday was our last full day. We had an enjoyable walk for a few hours from Rydal to Grasmere on a route called the 'coffin trail'. There were fab views and enough up and down to keep our legs active without being too taxing. By now we had started to feel a little sore in our legs from walking every day. After the walk, we drove to Ambleside and walked some more. When it started to rain, we found a nice pub with comfy chairs, and shared some food. A delicious crab ravioli with hand cut chips and a side of broccoli with almonds. It was one of the best meals of our trip.

When we got back to the B&B, we walked back into town to make the most of the evening as the evening tended to be the best part of the day. The sun had come out and it was just so nice to be outdoors and feel the sun on our faces. We walked up to the Belsfield Hotel which overlooks Bowness and Lake Windermere. The views are stunning from the terrace where we sat and shared a cream tea. After the scones, we didn't want to leave, so we ordered a glass of wine and a cheese board to share. We were there for hours, people watching and putting the world to rights. It was my favourite evening of the trip.

It was an imperfectly perfect trip. It may have rained almost constantly for four days. I may not have stuck to my rules on eating and drinking, but I spent four days quality time with the person I love the most, we had fresh air and exercise in a beautiful setting, and we laughed until our bellies hurt and the tears rolled. I feel so grateful for my life right now.

Reflecting on my time with Abi in the Lake District helped me when I completed the Personal Values Workbook Claire gave me for homework. My final list of Values are:

My Core Values:

1. *Health – without this I have nothing!*
2. *Trust – in myself and others.*
3. *Love – unconditional, unquestionable (Like I have with Abi.)*
4. *Having fun, laughing, being silly.*
5. *Being present, not being in the past or future.*
6. *Making a positive difference.*
7. *Learning – the process of learning.*
8. *Growth – different to learning; it's the outcomes related to development.*
9. *Team/Community/Belonging.*
10. *Accountability.*

What did you learn about yourself during the Values exercise?

- *I value how I feel more than what I have in terms of things!*
- *I've changed in the past six months!*
- *I feel happy about the changes*
- *These values feel more refreshing and more me at my HPS*

What were your biggest surprises?

- *I thought responsibility and independence would have been there. I think before the work with Claire, particularly on my parts, these would have been there and right at the top. I realise now that these would have been the values of my protective parts, not of my HPS.*
- *Trust was always going to be high. It is one of the reasons I could not accept my ex's lies. What I hadn't expected was for trust in myself to be part of the same value. I need to trust myself in order to have confidence in my trust in others. I trust myself when my HPS and not my parts make the decision to trust people. It was my lonely 'inner child' that chose my ex. It was my 'All Knowing Part' that didn't want to accept the signs he couldn't be trusted. My 'All Knowing Part' and my 'Critical Part' were often arguing inside me when something didn't add up. No wonder I felt I was going mad during those last few months with him.*

My Tribe

Now I have my Values I need to start thinking about growing my Tribe: people with similar core values. I already have these people in my Tribe:

Abi

Bridget

Dotty

Louise

Cheryl

Sian

I notice they are all women. I feel I need some greater diversity in my Tribe. I need to think about how I can find new people with similar core values but different backgrounds and perspectives to help me to continue to learn and grow. I think I will talk this one through with Claire.

Superpower Boost Morning Routine

My morning routine has developed as follows:

- *Drink a glass of water*
- *Write down five things I am grateful for*
- *Set my intentions for the day*
- *Move – five mins cardio (I hula hoop!) and five mins stretching*
- *Stand in front of a mirror, smile and say, 'You've got this!'*
- *Then once I am ready to work, I tackle or prepare for my hardest task of the day and I feel confident and accomplished*

I don't meditate. I leave that until lunchtime. It's good to give my mind a break by then and keep my day on track.

I usually reflect in my Journal on an evening. It helps me sleep if I get all of my thoughts and feelings out as part of my evening relaxation routine.

I am always learning. I love learning on the go using Audible for books. I have subscriptions to lots of podcasts Claire has recommended and I have found a few of my own favourites. I often combine my daily walks with a podcast or audio book or listen to them on the commute to work.

I've had this routine for a few weeks and it has me feeling in control of myself in a way that feels light and easy. I used to try to be in control by staying on top of everything, always thinking about what was on my plate and trying to second guess it and prepare for the worst case scenario. Now I feel much more relaxed and ready to deal with whatever comes my way. I trust my HPS to be enough. Wow! I hadn't realised how far I have come until writing that! Maybe the neurons are all firing in the right patterns now and I have actually made change happen. Maybe I am finally on my way to becoming 'Super Neuro Me'. It's not just a mantra.

Journal, Day 180 – Another great coaching session

We are on Zoom again today. It saves so much time and I feel more comfortable sharing some things over Zoom from the privacy and comfort of my own home. Claire asks me to reflect on my progress to date. It feels good to reflect out loud on my journey so far. It's been five months since I started the coaching and about six months since I separated from my ex. I feel I have come a long way and I am finding life to be easier and at the same time I feel I am achieving more at work and at home.

We talk about being realistic and accepting that there will be times when my HPS will not be as easy to access. Parts will still get triggered from time to time and I need to keep up all the good work to minimise their sensitivity. I share with Claire a good example of this which happened earlier this week. I am a bit embarrassed to share but know Claire won't judge me. I am disappointed in myself and want to understand what went wrong. Why hadn't I been my HPS? What happened to my superpowers?

I told Claire, "I thought I recognised her as soon as I walked into the bar. It was the ex-wife of my soon to be ex-husband. I had popped in for a drink before getting the train home from York.

"I had been in an all-day Board meeting. I had been bored and I was tired and irritable. The meeting could have taken a couple of hours and not all day. People clearly hadn't read their papers in advance and when I looked around, I felt like I was the only one who was prepared and focused. This annoyed me but I kept my angry part at a distance and remained patient throughout. I decided to stay curious and compassionate, perhaps they all had good reasons for not being prepared and I shouldn't judge. I made a note to talk to my boss about the meeting to see what he thought and to explore what we could do to have more effective meetings in future.

"Lunch was the typical buffet of white carb overload, not a lettuce leaf in sight. I wanted something healthy to eat after just sitting all morning. There was no time for a lunchtime walk, either. I decided to leave the room for some fresh air and grab a salad from Pret and sneak it back into the hotel we were using for the meeting. We were paying for a five-star hotel and yet I still had to go and buy some healthy food from elsewhere. This is another thing I want to talk through with my boss."

Claire listens patiently as I carry on with my rant.

"Anyway, the point is that I wasn't in a great mood. I was tired and irritable but at least I was pleased I hadn't shown my frustrations in the Board meeting. Instead, I wanted a quick large glass of red wine before getting my train home.

"I sat on my bar stool at the bar of the hotel next to the station and ordered a large glass of Malbec. I haven't been drinking much lately and after a few large swigs I could feel it working; I was lightening up. It looked as though Brae-lynn was also on her own. Perhaps she was also killing time before her train. I finished my wine quickly, ordered another and walked over to where my ex's ex was sitting...

"Two bottles of wine later, we were the best of friends. We talked about Fuckwit 90% of the time, which is under-standable as that was what we had in common. We shared our stories and so much of what we told each other rang true to our own experience. He is a pathological liar. We laughed until we cried, mocking him and all his weirdness.

"The biggest laugh came at the end of the night. I asked the barman, *'Would you mind taking a photo of us, please?'*

"Then to Braelynn *I said, 'Let's take this one for Fuckwit.'*

"Then, giving the broadest of smiles to camera, we both raised our glasses. Then I emailed the photo to my ex's work email to be sure he received it. I wrote 'The ex-wives club' in the subject line and attached the photo. It was very,

very gratifying and a perfect way to end what was a strange but fun night. When we left the bar, we hugged tightly and promised to keep in touch then left for our separate trains still laughing about the photo and the email."

When I finish downloading what happened to Claire. I still feel a little ashamed and disappointed in myself and at the same time I am curious as to what happened. I told her this.

Claire responds, "That's good, stay curious. What about this is making you feel ashamed, Laura?"

Claire asks this in a very neutral tone, without any judgement. She waits patiently and in silence as I engage with the feelings of shame to understand them better. This isn't a part of me that is ashamed. My HPS is ashamed.

I say, "It was wrong to send the photo. It was done out of anger and bad judgement fuelled by alcohol. When I woke up the next day I saw things differently. We all do things we regret from time to time. I regret sending the photo as I sent it to hurt him. I don't want to be that person. Sometimes we might hurt people by our actions. This is inevitable from time to time, but I sent that photo wanting to hurt him. I'm not proud if that."

Claire didn't say anything in response. I carried on.

"I have started to feel much lighter and easier in myself over the past few months. I don't want to live in the past. If

I live until I am in my 90s, I am now about halfway through my life and I have lived less than half of my adult life. I want to move forward and learn from the past without carrying baggage from it."

I feel better just for talking this out. Claire asks, "Laura, is there anything else you want to say about this?"

I sit back in my chair, drink some of my water and think for a while. "Yes, alcohol is bad for me when I am feeling negative emotions. It fuels them and encourages me to do things I might regret. When I'm in a good mood it fuels the good mood, but when I'm angry, frustrated or sad it just makes me worse. I need to avoid drinking when I feel like this."

"Okay, what can you do to manage your bad mood instead of turning to alcohol?"

I think, what would Wonder Woman do?

"I need to go to my superpowers. Do something to feel calm or creative or connected. I need to put into practice, 'Notice, Movement, Mood, New posture, Mantra'. After the Board meeting I should have walked off my frustration. I had been sitting all day and a walk, with some good music on or a good podcast, would have changed my mood. I could have gone shopping in York whilst killing time before my train. This would have distracted me. I didn't need to send the photo. It hasn't changed anything. Being angry with him won't change the past and living with the anger just infects my present and future."

Then Claire tells me something I haven't heard before and I love.

Snake Poison

"If a venomous snake bites you, the bite can kill you; this is what we tend to think... But it's not the bite that kills, it's the venom that lives in the body. Don't let this anger live in your body. Let go of the anger and you can live a healthier life."

CLAIRE WALTON

I feel a huge shift inside me. It sounds daft but I can feel as though a heaviness leaves my entire body. I take a deep breath to keep me grounded as I feel tears start to well in my eyes.

After a long silence, other than me blowing my nose and wiping my tears, I feel ready to speak.

"I want to live a healthier life. All the supplements and vitamins, good diet and exercise and everything else is a waste of time and money if I hold on to this anger. I choose to live a healthier life."

Claire puts her hand to her heart, I take this as she feels my pain and my need to move on. She gives me time to compose myself and eventually asserts, "Good, let's have a chat with your angry part and get her on-side with this choice."

We go through what is now a familiar process of finding my angry part. I'm finding this easy enough to do, now I am so familiar with it. With practise my parts seem to have come to trust me and I trust my HPS to be able to find the parts without them taking over me. I focus on the angry part. It looks like she's coming back from holiday. She has her suit-case with her. She's pleased to see me. She's been a little bored on holiday. She's ready for a fight on my behalf.

I stay curious. I want my little dragon to feel wanted but at the same time I want her to wait in future until I need her. I want her to wait until being angry is going to be helpful to me. Being angry at my ex and his faults is not helping me. After a few minutes of sharing these thoughts with my angry part I can sense she understands and just wants the best for me. She is happy to wait until she is called for. I tell her to listen out for danger and to nudge me if she feels I've missed something rather than taking over me.

Once we finish talking to my angry part, Claire asks me how I feel towards my ex.

"I feel sorry for him. I can't believe I'm saying this but I feel genuinely sorry for him. We were clearly not a good match and instead of him admitting this to himself and to me, he lied to make himself seem a good match. He possibly convinced himself we were. The reality is that with all the deception we were living a lie. This felt stressful for me and I'm thinking now that it must have felt stressful for him too."

"How do you feel inside, now that you see him this way?"

I notice my body and how it feels. Normally when I think about my ex I am all tense and my heart pounds, my chest and throat are hot and tight, and I spit out expletives like I am spitting out green acidic bile. Right here, right now, I feel calm, I have an inner quiet, I feel open and light and balanced.

"The best word to describe how I feel is *neutral*. I don't feel inclined to call him and ask how he is and tell him I forgive him. I just don't feel I want to use up any more valuable energy on hating him or even thinking about him. Do you think I should forgive him?"

Claire takes in a deep breath and exhales it. I get the feeling she has been here before. Perhaps not just with clients but maybe herself. I wait for her to tell me what to do.

"What do you feel would serve you best, Laura?"

There she goes again. Claire often does this. Just when I think she will give me some direction, she turns the question back on me. I also take a deep breath and exhale louder than I had expected to. I take a few. I scan my body and shift in my seat until totally present and engaging all my superpowers.

"I forgive him.... I don't particularly feel compelled to tell him, but I absolutely forgive him. It does not serve me at all to hold on to the anger and the past. We were clearly not a good match from the start. I am also partly responsible for the situation because I didn't see and accept what is now obvious. There were signs very early on and for reasons that I understand now, I didn't react effectively to those signs. There were parts of me that wanted so much what they thought he offered me, and they silenced the parts of me that were screaming out that he wasn't real, he wasn't honest and he just wasn't right for me.

"When I met him, I was in a very vulnerable place. I had been in a job where my boss was sexually harassing me and the guy I was seeing had been messing me around. My ex felt like he offered me protection from all of this. I thought I could have my happy ever after with him. I didn't cause him to lie, but I understand why he did. I think I was lying to myself about him and who he was. Understanding and accepting this is enough for me. I forgive him. I also forgive myself."

My sense of relief is huge. I feel like a huge weight has lifted from my shoulders and I can breathe properly again. A few tears roll down my cheeks. They are tears of relief, happiness and I believe they are going to be the last tears I shed about my short-lived marriage.

It was an intense session but one of the best feelings I have had for a long time. I feel energised and at the same time realistic. As Claire said, I need to expect ups and downs. Life is full of them. Doing all the exercises and good practices that boost my superpowers is going to help and I need to avoid those things that zap them. Claire gave me a few exercises to do when I feel my superpowers have been zapped. I will take a look at these later.

Before we finished, I asked Claire to help me think about how I can bring more diversity into my Tribe. Talking it though helps. I decide to try joining a dance class. This way I combine three things I value: exercise, learning something new and having a laugh. Claire recommended Salsa. She told me she had heard that Salsa classes attract single men so there might be a bonus element in this choice. Also, given the heritage of Salsa I am likely to meet more people of a wider ethnic mix. I decide it's worth a try.

Journal, Day 188

I have been awake for about an hour, after sleeping for about six. I'm sitting in the spare bedroom at Colleen's.

Colleen's house is like the Tardis. It looks like a twenty-foot wide, two-story house from the outside. When you get inside it's got an open plan lounge, kitchen and diner and upstairs there are four bedrooms and two bathrooms. I am sleeping in the spare with Isla. Isla is sound asleep.

She and Colleen had a lot to drink last night. Colleen had the most to drink, so much I stopped counting. I think at least a few bottles of champagne and cocktails before we left the house and then wine at dinner. She also ordered shots after dinner. I managed to get away with two glasses of champagne, one when I arrived and said yes out of politeness, damn my concern with pleasing others! The second was when Colleen ordered it at the bar last night before dinner and I was too polite to tell her no thanks.

It is so hard to be disciplined when I'm with other people. I enjoyed what I had but I am so glad not to have a hangover this morning. I don't know how I kept awake so late last night and I wouldn't have lasted until 1.30am had I been drinking at the same rate as the others. At one point when Colleen ordered coffee at about 12.30am I put my head on the table in fake/real sleep mode. I think she got the message as we left soon after.

Last night was lovely, though. Colleen took us to an amazing restaurant near the lake. It was a huge room converted from an old bank with high ornate ceilings, full of interesting looking people. The doorman had a cute top hat on, and I asked Isla to take a photo of me wearing it.

She said, "No, maybe later. I'm not drunk enough to ask him."

Interesting. I'm the one who gets accused of being boring for not drinking yet I was the one who so far had been singing.

I sang... "Money, money, money, it's a rich man's world," as we left the house and... "Stop right now, wait a minute, Mr Postman," as we entered the restaurant. I am also the one who brazenly walked up to the doorman and asked if I could wear his hat and have a photo with him. People often think you need alcohol to have fun. I don't. I just need to feel free and not stressed and I come to life.

The food at the restaurant was some of the best I have eaten. The salmon starter was so salty and bright pink. The sole was cooked perfectly, and the white chocolate mousse was heaven on a spoon. We didn't eat until about 10.45pm and by then I thought I was past eating, but the food was too good to pass.

I noticed that when Colleen speaks she speaks tends to speak to Isla and not me. I feel she is trying to impress Isla. When we were in the house, I thought this was because of the positions we were sat on the sofas, but last night at dinner she still spoke mainly to Isla. Colleen told us so many stories. The stories were so convoluted I lost track. Good job I'm not drinking much as I wouldn't be able to follow at all. It all sounds a bit far-fetched, but Colleen swears it is all true.

At dinner Colleen told us all about her long-standing affair with Richard. She shared how and why it started and many details about her life with her husband. I'm not sure what I think of all this. If everyone is happy then fine, I think, but are they? It all feels a bit of a compromise to me. I met Colleen's husband earlier that day and he looked like a broken man.

Isla also shared her stories of affairs whilst married to her husband, again both long-standing. I get why she did it, as she said her husband was awful and she only stayed with him for the sake of the children. I can relate to this, but I have no idea how people keep it going for so long. I had an awful marriage to Abi's dad but could not have had an affair because I'm a crap liar. Fitting in even a one night stand would have been difficult, meant nothing and would have made me feel rubbish about myself and guilty. I'm not judging anyone. Or am I? I think I may be. I know people have all sorts of challenges and I'm in no position to say what's right and wrong for them, I just know I don't like it and I'm starting to feel uncomfortable being party to these conversations.

I didn't feel very relaxed yesterday when Colleen challenged me on how many books I read. She said perhaps I should stop reading all these books and just have my own voice and tell my own story, and share lessons with others without feeling I need to read what she called, "So much bollocks written by others." She is entitled to her opinion but it's an opinion based on one book I mentioned to her that she hasn't even read. Without having read this book I think she has totally misunderstood me and what I do and why. I read because I want to get new ideas, apply them where I think it's worth it and reflect and learn from my own experience, where things resonate.

Journal, Day 191

How much being talked at can I possibly take! Colleen is just non-stop sharing stories, in great depth and with what I'm sure is huge exaggeration to 'entertain' us. Not only is she doing this, but because she was pissed last night she is telling us stories we've already heard. When I go to speak, even if it is in response to a question she has asked me, she will interrupt me or get distracted by something else and not listen to the answer. She just doesn't seem to care or realise she is doing it. She is so self-absorbed. I could not believe it when at one point this morning she talked about her high EQ. You have got to be fucking joking!

Isla seems oblivious to what is going on and just listens and is patient with Colleen when she interrupts her too. Colleen will ask a question and then start offering possible answers instead of me or Isla answering the question meant for us. Now, my dad does this sometimes but FFS he is a novice by comparison and thirty years older, which is somewhat of an excuse.

I spent the entire weekend practising all my superpowers and still it was exhausting. I have arrived home to my sanctuary of peace and quiet and I feel I can relax at last. Until this weekend I have found staying Calm, Clear, Confident, Courageous, Compassionate, Curious, Connected and Creative have helped me feel energised and at ease, so why am I so tired? Because I was staying with Colleen, I didn't feel I had Choice. I think this zapped all the other superpowers. It is so important to feel we have choices otherwise we can get dysregulated. In reality, I had a choice. I had a choice in terms of how I responded to the situation. On reflection, I fear I probably came across as standoffish and maybe even rude.

Coaching call

I called Claire to arrange a quick coaching call over the phone.

She says, "It sounds like whilst you were able to apply some of your superpowers, they were being zapped because you were not being yourself. What did your authentic HPS want to do that you didn't do?"

I think for a while.

"I was really trying hard to be my HPS all weekend. I tried so hard that I was exhausted. I really wanted to leave the situation, but it felt like that would have been rude. I didn't feel as though I was really being me, though, which also felt wrong. Maybe they could tell I wasn't happy. Don't get me wrong; there were some fun moments and some nice moments. Colleen was a generous host. I didn't always have the courage to say what I really thought and put it in a way that would serve everyone well. Instead, I kept my thoughts and feelings to myself and that was hard. After a while maybe I was 'leaking' what I was thinking without saying it."

"Now you are home and feeling relaxed, what other options do you feel you had that you didn't take?"

This is hard. I just wanted to run away from the situation. Based on that, I guess I wasn't applying all of my super-powers. I'm curious... what would Wonder Woman have done?

"I should have remembered Wonder Woman. I should have found the courage to be more curious, ask more questions and I should have shared my concerns and accepted the consequences. Worst case scenario, I could have left after doing this, booked into a hotel or taken an early flight home. I guess there is always an out and I felt trapped. I felt bullied. I allowed my 'inner child' to be triggered. It was like being a child again and having my brothers hold me down and fight me. I guess I've still got more practise to do on my superpowers."

Claire says, "No one is perfect! Even Wonder Woman sometimes gets it wrong and has to reflect and learn from her mistakes. On reflection, are Colleen and Isla people who you want as part of your tribe?"

"Collen isn't. She isn't a bad person, not at all. She just doesn't bring out the best in me. I'm happy to be challenged with a different point of view but not bullied. I have no ill will towards her, and she has helped me understand myself better. For this I am grateful."

Claire asks me if I have had a chance to complete the first superpower zapper exercise. I have to admit that I haven't. I have been busy with work and then with the trip to Zurich I haven't prioritised it. I think I might have been getting complacent with my homework because I have been progressing so well. The Zurich experience has taught me I am still a work in progress. I commit to myself to complete the exercises over the next week.

Journal, Day 192

I've completed the first superpower zapper exercise and here is my list.

My Top 10 Superpower Zappers[1]

- *Toxic relationships*
- *Giving in to temptation*
- *Imposter Syndrome*
- *Negative self-talk*
- *Negative thoughts*
- *Doing too much/overwhelm*
- *Ruminating on the past*
- *Comparing to others*
- *Too much challenge/too little challenge*
- *Disappointment when things don't live up to expectations*

Journal, Day 200

I have been working through the exercises Claire gave me which should help me with some of the superpower zappers I identified in Superpower Zapper Exercise One. These exercises are so simple and easy. I love them.

I started with ...

Toxic Relationships[2]

My Zurich experience has made me think about other relationships and who I am allowing to influence how I feel about myself. Claire has previously told me that my brain is energy hungry, using 25 watts of the available 95 the body runs off. I need to optimise energy for my brain! Any reduction in energy to my brain affects my performance. I don't want to waste any more energy on bad relationships. I have done enough of that lately with my ex. I want to move on and keep my focus on my new Purpose and my Vision of success in the future.

I have started the first action to build my Tribe by joining a local Salsa class. I've been to a few classes and I love it. I am useless which is what provides the laughs. I laugh so much sometimes my face aches. I have been partnered with a gorgeous guy. His mother is Spanish, and his Dad is from Yorkshire. He is a lot younger than me so I can't see any romance blossoming, but we have arranged to meet for coffee next weekend. It will be good to get to know him more and to see if he can be part of my Tribe. I like the idea of having younger people in my Tribe and his upbringing and his job are very different to mine. He seems to have similar values though, which is the critical element.

I have also started on my goal to build a Tribe at work. A coalition of people across the business who want to look at our culture through a lens of health. I've had tons of people express an interest in being involved and I want to make sure I have a diverse spectrum of people in the final cut for the team. I get excited whenever I think about what we can do together. This is why I need as much energy as possible these days.

I completed the Toxic Relationships exercise from Claire's website and identified a pattern. I tend to want to be everyone's friend. In terms of intent, I am a bit of a people pleaser. I seek approval. I want people to like me. I try so hard and bend and twist for people to like me and I don't tend to think too much about how they are treating me and if they are good for me. Going through the parts work with Claire has helped me understand that it is often my parts trying to protect my 'inner child' from being hurt again. 'Super Neuro Me' wants to stop these unhealthy relationships and allow my parts to stay on holiday and not to blend with me.

I have identified a couple of people I need to have conversations with to let them know why I intend to change the nature of our relationship. This is going to require my HPS and all nine superpowers to be fully activated.

I want to thank Colleen for the Zurich trip and let her know that I appreciated her generosity but tackle what I believe is the elephant in the room. I cannot pretend to be okay with her affair. I think this was at the heart of my response to her. I have just come out of a relationship full of lies and I cannot be around someone who is laughing about the lies she is telling her husband. I will feel better sharing this with her and wish her luck.

I also identified a toxic member of my team, who has been causing problems for me and the rest of the team over the past year. I have given her feedback and tried to help her with training and other support, but she isn't changing. I guess it's a bit like Claire says: 'You have to want to change.' I don't think Janet wants to change. I think she has been coasting slowly towards retirement for some time. My predecessor over-promoted her, and she has never achieved the requirements of the role. I have invested too much energy in her. This is energy I could be spending with other members of the team or with my new Tribe of culture change agents.

I have decided to have a final conversation with Janet to come to some agreement about her leaving. I have a meeting arranged tomorrow with Holly from HR to work through the details.

The Toxic Relationship Detox also helped me to identify who I need to moderate my time with and who I need to find more time for. It's a bit like how less sugar and more exercise will help me stay physically healthy: having less time with some people and more with others will help me be more emotionally and physically healthy. I am starting to see how some people encourage me (My Tribe) live to my values and others encourage me to compromise on my values and it is this that jars. Until now I have sometimes accepted this because I haven't had the courage to let them go, limit or change the nature of the relationship.

My recent mindfulness about what helps me and what hinders, boosts or zaps my superpowers, is making me see lots of things in a different light and the more I change just small things using Claire's exercises, the more I feel I am becoming 'Super Neuro Me'.

Giving in to temptation – 5 Second Rule[3]

In so many aspects of my life I am brilliant at discipline. But lately when it comes to my consumption of alcohol and sugar, I have found my willpower is weak. I am also allowing myself to stay up later and later at night for no particular reason. This makes me tired the next day, which stops me exercising in the morning and increases my desire for sugary foods. This chain reaction dilutes my superpowers.

In last week's coaching session Claire suggested the 5 Second Rule to manage this superpower zapper.

She says, "If you find yourself making to-do lists or setting intentions then not following through on them, the 5 Second Rule is brilliant. Knowing what to do and why you need to do it will never be enough."

Claire explains, "What you need is something that is going to launch you into action. It's no good sitting around waiting for motivation to appear out of thin air. Here's Mel Robbins' one-liner definition of the 5 Second Rule:

'If you have an impulse to act on a goal, you must physically move within five seconds or your brain will kill the idea.'

MEL ROBBINS

"For example, if you have a goal of making your ideas at work heard and acted upon, you must speak up next time you're in a meeting and you have a great idea. If you have a goal of losing weight, you must put the doughnut down and pick up a healthy snack or a glass of water instead.

"Whatever your goals are, get serious by taking action; however insignificant that action may seem, act now. When you take action, your brain starts to build new habits. When you do something you're not used to doing, you are in the act of building new habits and erasing existing ones. This is the neuroplasticity we have spoken about before.

"So, when do I use the rule?"

"The moment you feel an instinct or a desire to act on a goal or a commitment, use the rule. When you feel yourself hesitate before doing something that you know you should do, count 5-4-3-2-1-GO and move towards action. Counting backwards from five to GO is critical because there is a window between the moment you have an instinct to make a change and your mind killing the instinct. According to Mel Robbins, it is a five second window. If you don't take action on your instinct to change, you will stay stagnant."

"But if you count 5-4-3-2-1-GO and move towards action you can prevent your mind from working against you. You can start the momentum before the flood of thoughts and excuses hit you at full force."

I reply, "It's so simple. I still don't get how it works."

"The counting focuses you on the goal or commitment and distracts you from the concerns and excuses in your mind. As soon as you reach "1", you must literally launch yourself into action. This is how you push yourself to do the difficult stuff, things you don't feel like doing, or you're scared of doing."

It is really simple and after watching a Mel Robbins video on you tube explaining about the neuroscience of it, it made sense too. I used it a few times yesterday. I have been having great success so far, once to say no when a plate of cakes appeared in the Board room. I could see the plate coming my way around the table and I said to myself, "5,4,3,2,1 – Go." On Go I got up and walked over to the drinks table, poured myself a water and grabbed an apple instead.

When I got home after a long day I was tired from another day of meetings and wanted to just flop on the sofa. After taking off my work clothes I considered putting on my 'comfies' for a night on the sofa and instead said out loud, "5,4,3,2,1- Go," and threw on some gym gear and went back out of the house and to the gym. I was tired after the gym. I made a quick salad and watched some mindless TV and started to fall asleep on the sofa (this has become a bad habit). As I felt myself nodding off, I said very loudly, "5,4,3,2,1- Go," and launched myself off the sofa and up to bed for an early night. Super Neuro me!

Imposter Syndrome and 'Success Tapes'[4]

During several coaching sessions, I have been working with Claire on getting to know my 'inner child' and release her from her burdens and work with my 'protector parts'. However, I still occasionally feel self-doubt creep in and affect my confidence.

In our last coaching session Claire explained 'Imposter Syndrome' to me and an exercise that can help with this.

Claire says, "Lots of people suffer with 'Imposter Syndrome' or something similar. Imposter syndrome is loosely defined as doubting your abilities and feeling like a fraud. It tends to mainly affect high who find it difficult to accept their success and fear being 'found out'. Although women talk about these feelings more openly, research suggests men experience the same feels and to the same extent. Whilst a little self-doubt can be healthy and spur us on to prove ourselves wrong. Too much self-doubt can make us procrastinate, work too hard at something or it can stop us from trying something. Self-doubt and feelings of inadequacy can zap our superpowers.

When your superpower of confidence goes, calm, clarity, courage and creativity can follow. When this happens, we can apply self-compassion and connect with our curious self. We can ask ourselves, 'When did you earn the right to do this?' At this point we can go to our 'Success Tapes' to find the answer."

How to create your 'Success Tapes'

Success tapes help you internalise your success to remind your HPS that you have earned the right to be doing what you are doing, to have the role, status, recognition, promotion, or whatever other success you feel isn't yours to have.

Allocate a section of your Journal for keeping a note of your successes/achievements/wins. You might want to title this section, 'Success Tapes'

Then get the first page started by doing the following:

Think of a success/achievement/win you have had in life…

Now consider what made you able to achieve this win. Fill in the blanks:

I was able to …………………… because I ……………………………………

Now think of as many successes as you can and complete the process for each success.

Every day as you complete your Journal, see what you can add to your 'Success Tapes' list. When you add a new Success tape, read through all the previous ones too to remind you of all your recent successes and how YOU earned them.

I love this exercise. I've filled in pages already. It's like a constant reminder to my 'inner child' that she did well. She paved the way for me to achieve all of these things and be this person. I feel like I'm walking taller because every day I'm reminding myself of an old success or adding a new one. The thing about this exercise that makes the biggest difference is appreciating my role in my successes. My successes don't come by accident. It is because I am being or doing something to create that success. I have noticed when I answer 'because I...' it is often because I am being or enlisting one or more of my superpowers.

Negative Self Talk[5]

This was such a quick and simple exercise. Just by identifying some phrases I regularly use when I talk to myself, I
can change how I feel and what I do and as a result I have
better outcomes. The best example so far has been
replacing "I hate technology" when faced with a technol-
ogy-based problem with, "I love learning; what can I learn
about how to fix this?" I am using my values, the things
that matter most to me, as a way of reframing self-talk. In
this example I am using my value of learning to encourage
me to see the positive in the situation.

Negative Thinking[6]

I find I can get caught up in a negative thinking doom loop from time to time. It's normally when I have been doing too much, overstretching myself and I'm tired and frustrated. I start to make all sorts of small mistakes and everything seems to feel more difficult.

This exercise is another simple but effective way of getting out of the doom loop. I liked it so much I thought we could have some fun using it in my team.

At our team meeting on Zoom earlier this week I asked everyone to create their pack of 'Negative Thinking' cards. Then I got them into pairs and sent them off into breakout rooms to dispute each other's thinking. When they came back to the main room they shared some of their favourite examples. I've started to think that I want to use more of these exercises with my team as part of creating more of a healthy culture. The exercises that work well can be shared with the Culture Change Agents and we can look at how best to share across the company. We can reshape our lives for the better and have some fun doing it.

Journal, Day 215

I haven't exercised since a quick Pilates session on Monday evening. I just haven't been in my normal morning routine this week. Monday I was in Leeds too early to go to spin before work, and Tuesday I had a late meeting so I missed it again. Wednesday I had my hairdresser here in the evening, and Thursday I was working at an all-day Exec Team workshop in Manchester and had to be up at 5.15am so there was no time to exercise that day and I was way too exhausted when I got home. I'm also having a problem with my shoulder and neck since cycling over a pothole last week. There is always something getting in the way for me to get into good habits consistently.

I feel like I have a hangover most mornings and I'm not even drinking. I think I might be stressed without realising it. My sleep isn't great but I'm not lying awake all night, I just feel tired all the time. After feeling I had been turning things around, the last few weeks have made me feel like my old (and I mean old) self. This is not good. Yesterday in the team development workshop I listened to all sorts of sad stories in the session we had about 'getting to know people'. I kept thinking about how grateful I am that I am not grieving for someone. There was a lot about the death of a loved one in the session. I also heard people talk about their partner being their best friend and their rock. I've never experienced this.

I don't feel I have anyone I can totally lean on. My dad comes closest but he's getting old now, and whilst he does his best whenever I need him I couldn't tell him everything as I would worry about how it makes him feel. I love being with Abi but I couldn't burden her with exactly how I feel and it's not my place to be her best friend either; that's a role for her actual friends, people her own age. I am getting to a point in life where I feel I want someone by my side. Someone I can rely on to support me if I need it. Not that I'm planning on needing it. Dad won't be around for ever and whilst I've been through some tough times, as I age life is bound to present more. Also, now Abi has left home and is becoming more independent I want someone to rely on me too. I want someone to love and share life with. I want to be a rock as well as have a rock. I had hoped this could be my ex-husband.

I am starting to build my Tribe at work, and I've met a few like-minded people at the Salsa class. I met a lovely woman, Jane, who is a lawyer. We have been for coffee in Wetherby, and we swapped all sorts of good ideas about healthy eating and fun ways to keep fit. The problem is, I just don't have time to do everything. I have managed to book a lunch date in with Joe. We got on so well over our coffee date that we booked lunch for this weekend. I hope I'm not so tired I have to cancel.

I told Jane I had met Joe for coffee, and she said, "I knew you two had chemistry. Good for you, Laura."

She seems to think he fancies me. I doubt it; he's about fifteen years younger than me.

I am going to ask Claire for another coaching session. I will have to prioritise the time for it even though my calendar is stacked next week. I always feel better after a session. Claire always helps me work through my challenges so even if I'm sometimes two steps forward and one back, I'm always making progress.

Journal, Day 220 – Coaching Session

Claire responds to my download to her, "Sounds like you are taking on way too much. No wonder you're exhausted again. You know this, right? So, what do you think is going on inside you that is making you take on so much?"

Claire sits back into her chair, crosses her legs and waits for me to think. I take a few big breaths and let them out slowly. I move in my chair until I find a neutral position where my feet are flat on the floor, my shoulders are relaxed and my hands are relaxed on my legs. I think, 'Why am I taking on so much?'

I say, "I'm excited about my future. There is so much I want to do. It's not like I am doing things I don't want to do. It's quite the opposite in the main. I want to do my job, and lead on the culture change piece, and go to my Salsa classes, and meet up with my new friends as well as see Abi and my old friends, and follow my morning routines, and fit in some spin and Pilates classes in my free evenings."

Claire moves forward toward me. We are sitting in the corner of the hotel lounge again. It is busy with people carrying on their own conversations and I am not distracted I am drawn in by Claire. As she moves forward I do too.

"That all sounds very positive, Laura, but you are saying you're exhausted by doing all of this and then you going to be back to square one if you're not careful. When exhaustion creeps in, it affects your sleep, your mood and your capabilities. If you're not careful your morning routine will go out of the window, your eating habits will be affected, and you will start making other poor choices."

"I know, that's why I wanted this session. You're right, but what do I do?'

"Okay, firstly, I want you to try something. Don't worry, it won't make you look silly. I will do it too and we can do it seated. No one else will notice what we are doing. Are you up for it?"

I look around the hotel lounge. Everyone is getting on with their own thing. I nod back that I'm okay to have a go.

Claire says, "Put your arms out straight in front of you as though you are being an air steward about to point to the exits. Then take your arms out wide to point to the exits but reach your arms back as far as you can until they go out of your peripheral vision. Then stop them as soon as you can't see them any longer."

We both do this, and I notice that Claire's arms reach much further back than mine do.

"You can put them down now, Laura. When we are stressed and overwhelmed - doing too much - a sign of stress can be when we lose some of our peripheral vision. This indicates we may be overly focused. We miss things. We miss obvious things. We have a limited sense of reality and of what our options are. When we step back, slow down, create space and time to be calm and compassionate towards ourselves, we increase our peripheral vision. We will try this again at the end of the session when you have developed a little more calm and have accessed more of your superpowers. Okay?"

I'm fascinated and it makes sense. I agree to have another go at the end.

"First things first, Laura, you need to consider where your drive to do so much is coming from. Are you trying too hard to please everyone? You know there is a part of you that can sometimes take over and crave that feeling of being needed and wanted. Is this something that could be happening?"

I ponder on this for a while. Am I trying too hard again?

"Do you know, Claire, maybe I am a little. Maybe I'm so keen to make sure Jane and Joe become good friends and that my new Tribe at work stick with me, perhaps I'm setting myself unrealistic expectations and doing more than is necessary to keep people with me."

"Okay, great, if that's the case, what can you do about it?"

"Just stop it." I say it with a smile. Now that I have put my finger on it, I can just stop it. The coaching has helped me realise I do this and why I do this, and I've just had a word with myself and gently told myself to stop it!

Claire laughs in response. She's not laughing at me but with me and I feel the stress I have put myself under recently start to melt away.

"Laura, you're used to having too much to do. You wouldn't have got to your role at work had you not always had more to do than the time to do it. What have you done successfully in the past when this happens?

Good question…

"I prioritise based on return on investment and timing. What needs to be done now, because it has an impact on me or others now. What has to be done now because it will make a big impact in the long term. And what can wait."

"Okay, what do you do with what can wait?"

"I plan it in my diary for when I will have time to do it to make sure I don't lose sight of it."

"Great, is there anything else you would normally do in this situation?" Claire asks.

"I will often look to see if I can approach what I have to do in a more efficient way."

"Is there any opportunity to apply this approach here?"

I contemplate Claire's question. There must be, there always is. "I can outsource food prep for a while. Jane, the lawyer from Salsa, uses a local health food delivery service. Actually, that's something I should table at work. Perhaps it's something we could branch into. I tried one last year, but I still had to do the cooking. The one Jane uses sends them all prepared and to your calorie budget as well as your financial budget."

By the time I spent just thirty minutes getting curious with Claire about the principles of what I have tried before, I came up with all sorts of ideas to pace myself and make what I want to tackle now more efficient. My superpowers of calm, curiosity, clarity and creativity were on fire and I started to feel confident I could gain control over my world again.

Ruminating on the past[7]

I mention to Claire that I have also started to dwell a little too much on the past. After Jane got the wrong end of the stick with me and Joe, it got me thinking about moving forward and starting a new relationship with someone at some point in the future. The problem is that when I try to be optimistic about this I quickly shift into thinking about what went wrong with my ex-husbands. Claire suggests a number of approaches to this. We start by doing a quick version of the "Wheel of Awareness" to ground me in the present and to help me to apply calm, clarity, curiosity, self-compassion and connectedness to this element of my past.

I've been doing something similar, but different, when I think about what might be possible with my career now that I have renewed energy and ambition for that. Can I really do what is needed to be the next Global Commercial Director and sit on the Group Board? I start to wonder if this is just a pipe dream and I convince myself it probably is. Claire suggests I go back to my "Success Tapes" and "Negative Thinking Exercises" to help address my emotions and thoughts about the global role. Claire reminds me that the crippling self-doubt of Imposter Syndrome can come and go. Perhaps I need to be more consistent with the exercise and the same goes for the negative thinking. She's right, of course. When I start to feel good, I tend to stop doing my good practices and then the negative thinking and the self-doubt creep back. I am a work in progress!

Before we leave the session we do the exercise where we check our peripheral vision. I can move my arms so much further back this time. Claire was right. I can see so much more now that I have accessed my superpowers through the session with Claire – just by being with her, listening to the calmness and curiosity in her, feeling her compassion and receiving clarity from her knowledge. I feel more connected through the mindfulness exercise and I am confident I can do some things differently to stop being overwhelmed by too much to do.

My Homework

Claire also sent me home with some new homework to do – A worksheet on The Superpower of Choice and Saying No[8].

I will tackle that this weekend. I am going to tap into my superpowers of courage and choice and learn to say no more often. All too often I say yes, because I believe positive and helpful people say Yes and Unhelpful people say No. I know this is part of my problem. I need to work through this and Claire tells me the worksheet will help me do this.

Journal, Day 240

It was a good drive to Doncaster Racecourse, chatting all the way about work and boyfriends and life. Now I have sort of started seeing Joe, and Abi is seeing Dan, we have something new to talk about and it feels more positive for both of us. Having a grown-up daughter is such a blessing.

We met my friend Dotty there as she lives nearby. We were very understated and perhaps underdressed. I thought, "What the hell." We were comfy and warm, and when it got sunny we took off our jackets and we were cool. There were so many women dressed like they were going to a posh wedding or something and by 2pm they were a mess, shoes off and risking standing on something vile or dangerous in their bare feet. There were some amazing outfits going on but on the other hand there was some complete 'mutton dressed as lamb' going on too. Great for people watching, getting all judgemental and feeling good about yourself. I know Claire might say I shouldn't judge. I should be compassionate. But, hey, I'm human and I'm a woman and so it's natural, isn't it? I'm not an Angel, surely I can let my halo slip every once in a while.

Considering it had been a wet and cold week the weather was good. It was about twenty degrees and most of the time it was sunny. We had pre-ordered picnic boxes and collected them about 4.30pm. This was after we had indulged in ice cream which hadn't quite filled us. We eventually found a table sat near some guys dressed in suits, pissed and necking champagne like it was lemonade. They were full of themselves and talking bollocks. Having said that, we were grateful for the seats. Seats anywhere that day were at a premium.

We had five minutes to bet on the last race. We all bet separately and by coincidence we all decided on No 4, 'Jackwilldoit' or something like that. This was the first time we bet on the same race. So far none of us had won anything at all. We took our places on the stands this time to get a full view of the course. Our horse was at the back for about 4/5ths of the race and then from nowhere seemed to come up towards the front. In the last hundred metres, it was No 4 and No 1 racing each other. They went over the line and we had no idea if we had won. The big screen flashed up PHOTO FINISH between 4 +1. It took ages and then: WINNER... No.4. We jumped up and down and I temporarily forgot about my pelvic floor and the inevitable happened. I couldn't believe it: what a great way to finish the racing.

Reflecting on my day I realise that I do quite a lot of comparing myself to others. It didn't cause a problem today, but at work in particular it can make me feel less worthy, less capable and less happy. It's when I look at what someone else is doing and start comparing it to what I am doing that I start doubting myself again. It also happens when I look at social media. I see a post on LinkedIn and start thinking I should be posting more or thinking I will never get a promotion if I don't increase my profile. I fall into that trap where I believe everything everyone says and does and forget it might not always be 100% honest. I start considering that they might be compromising to do what I see them post about. I've been the same with Facebook and Inst lately. I see my friends doing well and I'm envious rather than happy for them. It's not healthy but I seem not to be able to stop.

Journal, Day 241 - Comparing to others

Coaching Call

I have a quick coaching call with Claire today. We talk about my issue with comparing myself to others. I knew it was one of my superpower zappers. I wrote it on the list I did ages ago, but it was down towards the bottom of the list. Now I've been working on the others and seeing some progress, I need to tackle this one.

Claire says she loves a C Word! But there are two C words in particular that she doesn't like and one is Comparison! She shared this quote:

"Comparison is the thief of Joy." "I think it's Theodore Roosevelt," she adds.

It is so true. I have been feeling really happy with myself lately. I am doing so well on so many levels. I am fitter and slimmer than I have been for ages. I haven't weighed myself because I have stopped compulsively doing that. Compulsive is another C word Claire has taught me to avoid. I am being Consistent though. Consistency is not a superpower as such but applying the routines, techniques and practices that enable superpowers requires consistency. Consistency is a good C word!

Claire suggests I might want to have a look at one of the books listed on her website called *Notes on a Nervous Planet*, by Matt Haig. I have already bought it and I've been dipping in and out of it. I think I will have a proper read of the chapter on social media as Claire recommends. Claire tells me Matt talks about how to stay sane on the internet.

Notes on a Nervous Planet, by Matt Haig

In a nutshell he says:

- Resist whatever unhealthy excesses you feel drawn towards
- No one really cares what you look like; they are too busy caring what they look like
- Understand what seems real might not be
- Don't play the ratings game (Likes on LinkedIn etc…)
- Don't spend your life worrying about what you might be missing out on
- Don't pretend to be who you are not

He has one page where he gives tips on "How to be happy". I love it; here it is:

How to be happy

Do not compare yourself to other people

Do not compare yourself to other people

Do not compare yourself to other people

Do not compare yourself to other people

Do not compare yourself to other people

Do not compare yourself to other people

Do not compare yourself to other people

MATT HAIG

It's true. When we compare ourselves to what others have, or simply how they are, we are essentially making ourselves feel less than we are. With social media as a platform to flaunt every aspect of our lives, high expectations that we will earn a certain amount, to own the latest whatever and to look a certain way it's inevitable we are going to zap our superpowers.

So, no more. If I feel myself start to compare rather than listen, observe and learn, I will stop and distract myself by doing something from my superpower boosts or just get on with something I enjoy. I was so glad I had a quick call with Claire to keep me on the right path.

Journal, Day 260

I visited my Aunt Susan in Doncaster today. She is eighty and she's had Multiple Sclerosis for a few years. She has got to the point of not wanting to live anymore which is sad but understandable as she has very little life going on these days. She is stuck in her flat most of the time and sitting in a chair which she also sometimes sleeps in. She needs to use a commode and cannot get out of the flat without someone coming for her and pushing her in a wheelchair. Carers come in three times a day to sort out meals for her but the boredom on top of the pain must be awful.

She was always such an active person too. I always remember her as the aunt who would bake constantly. Whenever we went to see her as children, she had baked fairy cakes and scones. She would always play cards with us and Scrabble. She would always win too. Her mind is still very sharp for someone of her age and I think this must make her situation worse for her. She has signed forms to say she does not want to be resuscitated in the event she stops breathing. Although this all sounds very sad, and it is, it was a lovely day.

Aunt Susan had booked a table at an Italian restaurant just around the corner and it was a good job it wasn't too far as it was difficult pushing her in the wheelchair. I hadn't thought it would be but there wasn't a ramp outside her flat and there were several steps to navigate. I thought I had pulled something in my back pushing and pulling the wheelchair, but I think I'm okay. She must have a ramp; I've made a mental note to speak to my dad about this later.

I have no idea how the carers manage as the one who called in whilst we were there was shorter than me and looked like if I blew on her she would fall over, yet somehow, she manages. I asked my Aunt about the ramp situation, and she said it wasn't easy. At one point, I had to call a neighbour and his wife to help me. I felt so sorry for Aunt Susan and kept making a joke of things as I could sense she felt humiliated by the situation. If she wasn't so heavy it would be easier, but because she can't walk she can't burn off what she eats, and because she is bored and fed up and can't cook for herself, what she eats is not that nutritious and is laden with calories.

The experience made me reflect that I must appreciate what I can do and how fit I am instead of often focusing on what I can't do. My issues are nothing when I think of my poor Aunt.

She loved getting out of her flat for a few hours and the meal was nice. She wanted the Tiramisu; she had been looking forward to it all week, once she knew I would be visiting. I was too full to have dessert and I'm still restricting sugar so wouldn't have had one anyway. Aunt Susan devoured the huge portion and loved every second and every bite of it. It was a joy to see her so happy for a while at least. We asked about takeaway deliveries and the waiter gave us the menu and said they could deliver without charge and the same delivery driver every time who would come into the house and serve it up for her. We took a menu.

I thought, what the fuck, it's too late now to worry about calories and if this makes you this happy Susan you should have one every day.

Seeing Aunt Susan made me contemplate my own life for the next thirty plus years. How do I want those years to be until I'm eighty like her? I want them to be full of life, positive experiences, good times with good people, fun, interesting and challenging. Hugging, laughing and loving with people I care about. Who knows exactly what this looks like, but I think I know how it feels... It feels like it feels when you're eating Tiramisu without a care in the world. Not caring about the calories, about what anyone else thinks and just wanting those few minutes to never end. I have been obsessing about calories and exercise lately and I need to be careful I'm not affecting my mental health and happiness by doing this.

Mini Coaching Session[9]

I share my reflections after Aunt Susan's visit in yesterday's mini coaching session with Claire. We start to work through managing more effectively all the things I want to do at work and with the rest of my life.

I explain to Claire, "I have completed the exercises you gave me for homework and I am getting so much better at staying focused on my purpose, values and vision of a successful future. I am prioritising better and saying No! and it is really making a difference. I don't want to get bored, and I don't want to have too much on my plate. I want the balance to be just right!"

Claire suggests I take a look at the exercise 'The Goldilocks Principle'.

This morning I completed the exercise and googled more about the principle. My curiosity about it had been piqued. This, is what I've taken from what I read:

Research indicates some stress is good for you and too little stress can be bad. There is something known as stress related boredom and this leads people to engage in counterproductive behaviour such as spending aimless time on the Internet for non-productive reasons, bitching about colleagues, leaving less time to complete productive tasks or rest, relax or have fun.

Whilst my excessive stress has previously led to mental exhaustion and poor health, not enough stress is likely to result in boredom and demotivation. Not only is this useful to me personally but also to me as a leader. For my individual benefit and for the benefit of those that I lead I need to apply The Goldilocks Principle.

The Goldilocks Principle

Where the optimal level of stress is not too much, not too little, but an amount that's just right.

I have concluded:

Set challenging, yet realistic goals.

For myself, my team and others I influence indirectly, I need to make sure I am not being impatient and a perfectionist. Instead, I need to agree goals that are challenging and at the same time achievable. An unrealistic expectation is likely to cause me to feel demotivated and disappointed and then likely to look for unhelpful ways of making myself feel better. I remember the Reward and Acquisition arrow on the HPS laminate Claire gave me in one of our early coaching sessions. When we feel unhappy we can reach for the instant gratification of things like unhealthy foods, alcohol, retail therapy and so on.

It's the same with deadlines. Unnecessary and unrealistic deadlines create a false sense of urgency. Working to a ticking clock raises cortisol levels. Whilst we all work well under a certain amount of pressure, it is about getting that level just right for each of us. We also have to look at each deadline against everything else that we have a deadline for. It's a bit like coaching with Claire. When she asked me to do the Superpower Boost exercises and the Zappers, she didn't ask me to do them all at once. Because of this I have completed all of them. If she had given me too many at once I might have been put off and not done them at all. Goals should be challenging and at the same time realistic.

Provide regular feedback.

Am I doing a good job? Is what I am doing getting me closer to achieving my goals. Is it making me happy? Am I making my boss happy? Lack of feedback creates doubt, which, in turn, creates unnecessary stress. Stress increases the pressure to perform and then performance anxiety can creep in which almost always makes your performance more unlikely.

Much like in the children's story Goldilocks, I need to find the level of stress that is 'just right' for me and my colleagues to perform at our best.

High Expectations and the Unexpected Joy of the ordinary

In today's coaching session, we speak about my high expectations for being happy and how sometimes I can, as we all can, expect too much from life. Then, this makes me disappointed with life and with myself and others.

I tell Claire, "My visit to Aunt Susan's and seeing her get such pleasure from the Tiramisu made me feel like I want more 'Tiramisu moments' in my life. You know, just the simple pleasure of not giving a fuck."

"Laura, I recommend you read *The Unexpected Joy of the Ordinary* by Catherine Gray. I devoured this book over a weekend. Catherine talks such good sense, and she has such an easy writing style. Some of the book reinforces some of the work I have already covered with you. Reading this will help you find more of those 'Tiramisu moments' for yourself. Did you know, research studies by the Office of National Statistics have shown that the happiest age group is age 70-74?"

"My Aunt is eighty and very sick, but my dad is 74 and still very fit and well. Dad has certainly been happier in his more senior years."

Claire recommends, "You might also find this interesting..."

The Top Five regrets of the dying :

1. I wish I'd had the courage to live a life true to myself, not the life others expect of me
2. I wish I hadn't worked as hard
3. I wish I had had the courage to express my feelings
4. I wish I had stayed in touch with my friends
5. I wish I had let myself be happier

Bronnie Ware, *The Top Five regrets of the dying.*

I say, "It's quite sobering. I notice the superpower of courage comes up a couple of times."

"Courage relates to being yourself and expressing what you need. Staying in touch with friends is an element of staying Connected. Friends, real friends, our Tribe, are a critical part of our support system, keeping us superpowered. Number Five relates to Self-Compassion."

In the past I have found myself striving for things that didn't make me happy. Sometimes it was the striving itself that didn't make me happy. It's back to the Return On Investment (ROI) principle again, the unhappiness of the striving outweighed the value of the outcome I was striving for.

"I wish I had known all of this when I was younger. I would love to share all these lessons with younger women. I have started sharing some of the lessons from my coaching journey with Abi as well as with my team at work. I feel like by sharing I am getting even more value for money from the coaching. I'm also just compelled to share what works well.

Claire responds in appreciation for the feedback with a huge smile. I go on, telling her about the 'What Works Well approach' we are using in my team.

"I picked this idea up from the Caroline Welsh book, *The Gift of Presence – A Mindfulness Guide for Women,* you recommended. She quotes the three W's as coming from Rich Fernandez, CEO of Search Inside Yourself Leadership Institute."

Questions we have been asking are:

- What have you been learning about?
- What has worked well for you?
- What specifically are you doing differently?
- How is this Making A Difference, for you and for others?

- I have become thirsty for self-improvement and ways to improve my team and my organisation over the past eight months or so since the coaching started.

My Homework

At the end of our coaching session Claire recommends some more homework.

What brings me joy? [10]

I will have a look at this at the weekend. In the meantime, I have another meeting with my culture change agents today. I am so excited because we are putting final plans together for a presentation to the Board. Now that brings me Joy!

I also I have a date with Joe. He also brings me Joy. He also keeps me on my toes! There is no comfort zone when it comes to dating a man fifteen years younger. I have even more motivation to stay healthy and fit and happy now.

Journal, 3 Years later

What an amazing day! The final day of our first global 'We Women are Making A Difference' Programme. I feel so proud. We have had 250 female leaders from across the organisation complete a twelve-month programme to develop them into more confident and capable leaders both within our organisation and beyond. The programme is based on helping our female leaders find their Highest Potential Self through development of their superpowers. As part of the programme, they take the lead on local or global projects to Make A Difference across the organisation.

They graduated. It was like a proper graduation, certificates, badges and everything. Where people could travel, they came here to our office in Los Angeles. They loved the renamed Corporate Headquarters, now called 'Heart of Life', part of the rebranding of our Company to 'Life'. We fundamentally sell the same things, but we sell them differently and we have a different way of doing business and treating employees, customers and other partners. This culture change started when I put my Tribe together three years ago as part of my actions from my coaching with Claire.

My first coaching session seems like a lifetime ago. I feel like I am my Highest Potential Self now. I don't have to try to be it; I am so well practised that it is who I am now. I feel like my 'inner child' has been totally healed and my protective parts have no need to step in and take over. I am grateful for all they did for me before I learnt how to access my superpowers and further develop them to stay in my HPS. After eighteen months of regular coaching sessions with Claire, I decided I wanted to share my lessons with others. Claire introduced me to the 'MAD Ripple Effect'. I wanted to not only role model the superpowers, I wanted to share them with other people. We have started with female leaders because our female leaders are under-represented across the company. It is my aim to encourage more women to have the confidence that they can achieve more success for less stress. The superpowers bring this ability.

Since working with Claire, I have found I can achieve so much more than I ever did before. I am much less stressed. Any stress I have is positive stress that spurs me forward and energises me to achieve more. The changes I made whilst working with Claire have made me a better person, a better mum, a better girlfriend and a better leader. My success at work is something I feel good about as it no longer comes at a cost. I am able to achieve success across all aspects of life at the same time. My life is integrated; I am integrated.

Claire is still my coach. I see her regularly for coaching but not quite as often, as I have become much more self-sufficient. Our sessions are incredibly valuable. The sessions help me to reflect and be held accountable, to keep me on track with my goals and learn from my experience. I still go back to some of the exercises from time to time. I am 'perfectly imperfect' and sometimes fall off the wagon a little. The various exercises Claire gave me help me get back on track in between my coaching sessions. I have maintained my morning routines, my daily six-Minute Reflection activity, and I have several Pilates sessions a week. We run these at 'Heart of Life' which makes my life easier. No excuse not to attend. I hike in the L.A. hills and Joe has taught me to surf. I couldn't be happier.

I am writing in my Journal now because I plan to be a little too merry to write later. We have our Graduation Gala this evening. I am on the top table with Claire, Abi and Joe. It is quite a family affair. Claire is there, obviously, as the facilitator for our 'We Women are Making A Difference' programme. Abi was the internal lead on the programme. She joined 'Life' eighteen months ago to help with the culture change programme. Joe is there because we value the partners of our colleagues. In our culture we appreciate the partners who support our colleagues to be at their best for us. We encouraged all of the participants to bring their partners to the Gala.

I need to go. Joe is calling me.

Joe is out on the deck waiting patiently for me to get ready. As I walk into the open plan lounge of our beautiful beach front house, I notice sand on the white wooden floorboards. He's done it again. He always leaves a trail of sand on the floor after coming in from a run on the beach. I have learnt not to complain. Not to be so perfectionist about things. Some things just do not matter. What matters is that I have a fit, young, gorgeous man waiting to take me to the Gala. I notice he has two champagne glasses waiting on the table on the deck and a bottle of champagne chilling in a bucket.

I am reminded of the scene I imagined in the exercise with Claire almost four years ago. I have worked hard to get here, and it has all been worth it. I have Made A Difference for myself, for my team and for my organisation.

I hope this book inspires you to do the work you need to do to make a difference for you and for others. You can achieve so much more for yourself and others when you start by finding and developing the nine Superpowers that enable your HPS. Calm, Clarity, Curiosity, Compassion, Creativity, Courage, Connectedness, Confidence and Choice are your Superpowers. But every one of us is unique. Every one of us has a unique story which drives our Purpose. Your story boosts your Superpowers. I once read, 'Your struggles are your power." I believe this can be true if we own our story as a positive force to fuel us to Make A Difference for others.

How has Laura's journey inspired you? What difference do you want to make for yourself?

What difference do you want to make for others? Do you want to be a better parent, friend, or colleague? Do you want to be a better leader at work or in your community? Perhaps all of these.

Since she was eight years old, I have been telling my daughter that freedom lies in the choices that she makes. Choices are empowering. Sometimes we feel stuck, with no choice or very little choice, but this is simply never true. There is always something we can do to change a situation even if it is just to change the way we feel towards the situation. We always have choices. Believing in this and applying this to our thinking and our actions is possibly the greatest of all Superpowers.

So, what do you choose to do now?

Having spent my first career working in very commercial organisations focused on profit and shareholder return, I became very familiar with the concept of Return On Investment (ROI).

Your investment in this book is far more than the sum you paid to buy it. It is in the time you have taken to read and engage in it. What return are you going to achieve for this investment?

In my second career as a High-Performance Coach, I also recommend clients consider ROI for their investment in coaching. Once again, their investment is so much more than in the fee for coaching sessions. You read in Laura's journey how she did her homework. She put into practice the insights she gained from the coaching sessions. She reflected both as part of her journaling as well as through more structured reflection activities. She was prepared to be vulnerable and open and honest with her coach, and she reached out for support from others to help her make the changes she wanted for herself. If we want to change, we have to invest the effort and have some patience with ourselves.

We can all change if we want to. Neuroscience has proven this to us. Our neuroplasticity means that we can rewire new physical, thought, emotional and behaviour patterns to achieve new outcomes. It requires help, practise and patience. Clients are not always patient. They want results immediately. We have become a society of people craving instant gratification.

The people we have become wasn't instantaneous. Becoming a better version of ourselves also won't happen immediately: it takes practise.

I often share with impatient clients the example of learning to drive a car. When we were younger, we looked at those who could drive and probably thought it was easy. We expected to have a few lessons and become excellent drivers. Learning to drive a car takes time, usually months. According to the RAC, "The average learner needs twenty hours of practice to pass the driving test, in addition to 45 hours of driving lessons." For those of us who have passed our driving test, we also know that passing our test is just the first stage of becoming a good driver. If you have been driving for years like I have you will also know that from time to time we become bad drivers because we become complacent, forget the basics and have accidents. Driving a car will always require effort and will sometimes require retraining.

Being able to drive a car opens up the world and creates more choices. It's a worthwhile Return On Investment. When I was seventeen, it took me six months, many lessons and many more hours of practice to pass my test. Since passing, I have had several small accidents and I have had to attend refresher training. The ability to drive brings us more choice and, at the same time, risks. As drivers we need to continue to apply what we have learnt to manage those risks.

Life comes with choice and risk. As a leader in life, be it in a parental role, in your job, or in your community, we need to make sure we are also fully competent. To do this I recommend continual development and a coach is a critical element of this. Find someone you have great chemistry with, that you like, you trust, and you can be yourself with. Be prepared to be vulnerable and open minded and be prepared to practise, practise, practise.

Go MAD; Make A Difference!

ABOUT THE AUTHOR

Let me help you Make A Difference

There are several different ways for me to help you and your organisation make a difference.

I coach individuals, teams and groups, design and run workshops, and speak at events.

Popular topics include:

- 'Super Neuro You' – Achieving more success for less stress

- Coaching for performance and potential
- Building and maintaining trust
- Conversational Intelligence - including how to have brilliant performance conversations
- Resilience for the 21st Century
- Leading people through the change rollercoaster
- Leading people in a pandemic
- Finding your purpose and creating a vision of success
- Finding your core values and developing your tribe
- 'Super Neuro Teams' - Leading high trust /high performance teams
- Women in leadership
- Embracing diversity

This is not an exhaustive list. I listen to your needs and provide bespoke solutions to meet them. I can do this independently or in collaboration with members of your internal HR and OD team, other suppliers of yours and other associates of mine.

I can also provide a variety of psychometric tools for assessing, thinking styles, leadership impact, group dynamics and culture.

All my services can be provided online and 'in person'.

I am a qualified coach and a member of a recognised professional body for coaches, The Association of Coaching.

You may have read some of the client testimonials earlier in this book. Any of these clients are happy to talk to you about their experience of working with me and the difference this has made.

If you would like to hear more from me or my clients please contact me.

I look forward to hearing from you.

Coach & Author

in linkedin.com/in/clairewaltonchangeagent

instagram.com/leadersaremad

facebook.com/leadersaremad

twitter.com/leadersaremad

REFERENCES

Chapter 3

- (Burnett, 2017)*The Idiot Brain: A Neuroscientist Explains What Your Head is Really Up To.*
- Dr Kristin Neff's Self-Compassion assessment https://self-compassion.org/test-how-self-compassionate-you-are/
- Self-Compassion Guided Meditations – https://self-compassion.org/category/exercises/#guided-meditations

Chapter 4

- Dan Siegel - The wheel of awareness. https://www.wheelofawareness.com/

- Amy Cuddy – Ted Talk https://www.ted.com/talks/ amy_cuddy_your_body_language_may_shape_who_ you_are?language=en
- Amy Cuddy - Presence - Orion (28 Jan. 2016)
- The process of 'Notice, Movement, Mood, New posture, Mantra' used in this chapter is inspired by training I have received from Amanda Blake. Find out more about Amanda and the many fantastic books she has written, go to: https:// embright.org/mandy/
- The coaching approach used in this chapter is inspired by a therapeutic approach developed by Richard C. Schwartz, Ph.D. - The Founder of Internal Family Systems. For more information on IFS go to: https://ifs-institute.com/

Chapter 5

- Jo Dispenza, Evolve Your Brain: The Science of Changing Your Mind Paperback – Illustrated, 1 Mar. 2009, Health Communications Inc
- https://provine.umbc.edu/books/laughter-a-scientific-investigation/
- https://www.psychologytoday.com/intl/articles/ 199607/happily-ever-laughter
- https://thethirty.whowhatwear.com/what-happens-to-your-brain-when-you-laugh
- The process of 'Notice, Movement, Mood, New

posture, Mantra' used in this chapter is inspired by training I have received from Amanda Blake. Find out more about Amanda and the many fantastic books she has written, go to: https://embright.org/mandy/

- The coaching approach used in this chapter is inspired by a therapeutic approach developed by Richard C. Schwartz, Ph.D. - The Founder of Internal Family Systems. For more information on IFS go to: https://ifs-institute.com/

Chapter 6

- Brene Brown, *The Gifts of Imperfection,* Vermilion (11 Oct. 2018)
- Brene Brown, *Daring Greatly, How the Courage to Be Vulnerable Transforms the Way We Live, Love, Parent, and Lead Paperback,* Penguin Life *(3 Dec. 2015)*
- Brene Brown, *Rising Strong,* Vermilion (27 Aug. 2015)
- Brene Brown, *Braving the Wilderness: The quest for true belonging and the courage to stand alone,* Vermilion; 1st edition (12 Sept. 2017)
- Brene Brown, *Dare to Lead. Brave Work. Tough Conversations. Whole Hearts.* Vermilion (11 Oct. 2018)
- Emilie Le Beau Lucchesi, *The Unbearable heaviness of clutter,* New York Times – Online, (Jan. 3, 2019)

- https://www.nytimes.com/2019/01/03/well/mind/clutter-stress-procrastination-psychology.html
- Miles Landry, BA, BS, Adriana C. Dornelles, ScD, Genevieve Hayek, BA, MS, Richard E. Deichmann, MD, *Patient Preferences for Doctor Attire: The White Coat's Place in the Medical Profession*, The University of Queensland School of Medicine, Ochsner Clinical School, and the Center for Health Research and Department of Internal Medicine, Ochsner Clinic Foundation, New Orleans, LA
- A range of studies conducted by sociology professors James Fowler and Nicholas Christakis clearly show that the health and wellbeing of one person affects the health and wellbeing of others in the same social networks.
- https://www.edge.org/conversation/nicholas_a_christakis-james_fowler-social-networks-and-happiness
- Gauri Sarda-Joshi, *7 ways your clothes change the way you think* - – Brain fodder - online
- https://brainfodder.org/psychology-clothes-enclothed-cognition/#:

Chapter 7

- 5 Second Rule - Mel explains more of the neuroscience of the 5 second rule - https://

melrobbins.com/5-second-rule-hack-science-explained/

- Matt Haig, *Notes on a Nervous Planet*, Canongate Books; Main edition (28 Feb. 2019)
- Bronnie Ware, *The Top Five regrets of the dying: The Top Five Regrets of the Dying - A Life Transformed by the Dearly Departing*, Hay House, (2012)
- Caroline Welsh book, *The Gift of Presence – A Mindfulness Guide for Women*, Scribe (19 Mar. 2020)
- Rich Fernandez, CEO of Search Inside Yourself Leadership Institute.
- Catherine Gray, *The unexpected Joy of the ordinary*, Aster (26 Dec. 2019)

RESOURCES

Introduction

1. All the Resources referenced can be downloaded from https://www.leadersaremad.co.uk/super-neuro-you/ using the password: SuperNeuro2021:)

3. Highest Potential Self

1. A Grounding Exercise to enable presence and support creative thinking
2. Vision of Your Ideal Future

Highest Potential Self - continued

1. Highest Potential Self Illustrations
2. Daily Reflection Activity
3. Dr Kristin Neff's Self-Compassion assessment https://self-compassion.org/test-how-self-compassionate-you-are/
4. Self-Compassion Guided Meditations – https://self-compassion.org/category/exercises/#guided-meditations.

4. Laura's Protector Parts

1. Wholehearted Listening - An Exercise to centre your mind and body
2. The wheel of awareness. https://www.wheelofawareness.com/.

5. Laura's Inner Child

1. Priming Exercise
2. HPS Progress Review
3. Self-care Checklist

6. Superpower Boosts

1. Purpose
2. From Vision and Purpose to Goals
3. Power up your home environment
4. Power up your wardrobe
5. Core Values
6. Superpower morning routine

7. Superpower Zappers

1. My Top 10 Superpower Zappers
2. Toxic Relationships
3. Giving in to temptation – 5 Second Rule
4. Imposter Syndrome and 'Success Tapes'
5. Negative Self Talk
6. Negative Thinking
7. Ruminating on the past
8. The Superpower of Choice and Saying No
9. Goldilocks principle
10. What brings you joy?

THANKS TO MY TRIBE!

I want to thank all those that have supported me in writing this book and getting it to the point of publish. To my daughter Emily, who inspired and encouraged me to write the book. To my boyfriend Jay, who listened and listened and listened before during and no doubt after publishing as I talked non-stop about ideas, the process, the problems and the opportunities.

To my family for bringing me into the world and being there when I ask for help.

I would like to thank my very good friends, clients and supporters for egging me on to write this book.

In particular I want to thank my friends, Susan Fulton, Helen Molloy, Dorothy Matthew and Rachael Elliott for always being encouraging and challenging in my endeavours to write, coach and be Super Neuro me!

I would like to call out some loyal clients who have trusted me again and again. In particular, Gareth Thomas – People & OD Director Brandon Trust, Bob Andrews – CEO Benenden Health, Lorraine Masters – Deputy Director Organisational Development Northumbria University, Sharon Lane – MD Tees Components, Andrea Malcolm – Executive Director, Bernicia Group, Lisa Davidson – Chief People Officer Connect Health, Helen Smith – Chief Commercial Officer Co-op Life Service, Rob Phillips – Group Finance Director The BBI Group, Matt Prosser – Technical Director Angel Trains, Ann Corbyn – Executive Director, people & Organisational Development Hertfordshire Partnership University NHS Trust, Debi Bailey - There are too many clients to mention all of you. I am grateful to have the opportunity to work with so many amazing Leaders, their teams and their Organisations. Thank you for trusting me to Make A Difference (MAD) alongside you.

I would like to thank the various coaches and therapists I have been helped by over the years. In particular, Deborah Kingston – Clinical Psychologist Psychological Therapeutic Solutions, Sile Walsh – Walsh Coaching and Consulting and Liz Calvert – IFS Therapist & Counsellor.

The illustrations in the book, on the cover and on my website are created by a fabulous artist, Ben Nightingale – Babatat Studio. Thanks Ben, you somehow manage to take the thoughts from my head and recreate them on the page.

My website and the inspiration for the book cover design comes from Nick Danks – Madhouse Media. Thanks Nick for always being so patient with me and all things technology, you have the patience of a saint!

Finally thank you to Abigail Horne and the team at Authors & Co. Writing a manuscript is one thing, transforming it into a book and getting it out into the world is a whole different story (forgive the pun). Thank you for being patient and kind and knowing your stuff!

There is a well-known proverb, 'It takes a village to raise a child'. I am a product of my village, not the town I group up in but the people who have influenced me throughout my life, my career, and now my book writing journey. Thank you from the bottom of my heart!

Claire Walton
Coach & Author

Lightning Source UK Ltd.
Milton Keynes UK
UKHW050211191122
412430UK00006B/150/J